Listen to me, I'm ANGRY

Listen to me, I'm ANGRY

by Deidre S. Laiken & Alan J. Schneider

Illustrated by Bernice Myers

Lothrop, Lee & Shepard Books   New York

Printed in the United States of America.
First Edition
1 2 3 4 5 6 7 8 9 10

Library of Congress Cataloging in Publication Data
Laiken, Deidre S
    Listen to me, I'm angry.
    SUMMARY: Advice for teenagers on how to cope with their angry
feelings and the anger of others directed toward them.
    1. Anger—Juvenile literature.   2. Adolescent psychology—Juvenile lit-
erature [1. Anger.   2. Psychology]   I. Schneider, Alan J., joint author.
II. Title.
BP575.A5L34   158   79-23406
ISBN 0-688-41943-7   ISBN 0-688-51943-1 lib. bdg.

THIS BOOK IS DEDICATED TO:

SAM, BLANCHE, AND LLOYD SCHNEIDER—

WHO KNOW WHAT LISTENING AND LOVING

ARE ALL ABOUT.

ACKNOWLEDGMENTS

The authors thank the following people who helped to make this book a reality: Dr. Malvina W. Kremer and Dr. Lawrence Balter for their time and patience. The children of the Hudson School in Hoboken, New Jersey, for sharing their feelings and fantasies. Dr. Barbara Chasen and Dr. Louis Berkowitz for their skill and insight.

CONTENTS

1. WHEN YOUR "COOL" BEGINS TO THAW 11

2. IT'S MY RIGHT! 16

3. IT'S ONLY A MOLEHILL, SO WHY DOES IT FEEL LIKE
   A MOUNTAIN? 26

4. RED HOT AND READY TO FIGHT! 36

5. THE ANGER YOU DIDN'T KNOW YOU HAD 46

6. ANGRY FANTASIES 59

7. LOVE MEANS SOMETIMES HAVING TO SAY "I'M
   ANGRY" 71

8. THE OTHER SIDE OF DISHING IT OUT . . . TAKING IT 89

9. COPING 104

10. ACCEPTING YOURSELF 119

    FOR FURTHER READING 121

    INDEX 123

Chapter One

WHEN YOUR "COOL" BEGINS TO THAW

No one likes to get angry. It doesn't look good and it feels even worse. "Keeping your cool" means a lot more than lowering your body temperature. It means never getting angry.

But, if you're a teenager, this isn't so easy because, at this time in your life, you probably have a lot to be angry about. One day you might be furious at a friend, a teacher, a parent, or your brother or sister. You might even be angry at your own body for not doing what you want it to do. All this makes "keeping your cool" pretty impossible. So every once in a while (or more) you let it all out. You blow up, shout, say a few things you might be sorry about later, and maybe you even throw something. Other times you hold it in, act "cool," and hope that if you ignore it long enough, the anger you're feeling will just go away.

Well, it doesn't go away. Anger has a very sneaky way of turning up at the strangest times, and in the strangest ways. And the more you try to avoid it, the more confused and out of touch with your feelings you become. You can think, for example, you are sad, tired, or sick, when, in fact, these feelings are really caused by an old anger that won't "just disappear." If you think that anger is just a matter of slamming doors or throwing punches, plates, and tantrums, you're only seeing a very small part of the picture.

THE OTHER SIDE OF ANGER

What else is there to anger? Plenty. Take Elaine, sitting alone in her room. She just slammed the door in her little sister's tear-stained face. What did her sister do? Nothing. Elaine just wants to be alone. She wants to get lost in her own little world. She has just put on her stereo earphones and is trying desperately to blast her way into oblivion. And instead of applying the special medicine for her troublesome complexion, her usual after-school routine, Elaine is eating chocolate bars. But not just one or two. She's now up to her fifth Almond Joy, undoing three weeks' worth of careful dieting.

Elaine isn't exactly having a good time. In fact, she's

miserable. She hates herself for eating candy bars and yelling at her little sister. No matter how much she turns up the music, it still doesn't make her feel better. But if you told Elaine she was angry, she'd probably think you were crazy. After all, she is sitting calmly and she isn't shouting or throwing anything. So how could she possibly be angry?

A better question might be what could Elaine possibly be angry about? You won't find out by asking Elaine because she obviously doesn't even realize that she's angry. But if we take a look at her day, her stereophonic candy binge might begin to make sense.

THE BLOWUP

Only a few hours ago Elaine was on top of the world. She woke up feeling this would be a special day. She was wearing a new sweater and really felt wonderful. Usually self-conscious about her skin, she was sure that today she saw some improvement and was feeling extraordinarily confident.

When she arrived at school, her friend Susan was waiting for her in front of homeroom. Susan and Elaine share everything—including Elaine's feelings of inadequacy about her complexion and her romantic interest in her classmate Lloyd. As the two girls talked and waited for the bell to ring, Lloyd stopped by. He seemed especially interested in talking with Elaine. (She was right, this was her lucky day.) As he was about to leave, Lloyd noticed Elaine's sweater and complimented her.

At that point Susan blurted, "Yeah, it's spotted—just like her face!"

Elaine froze. The bell rang, and it was time to go to homeroom. Susan turned to Elaine and whispered, "Hey, I was only kidding. Can't you take a little joke?" Not wanting to be a spoilsport, Elaine said nothing. But the rest of her day was terrible. Her attention drifted in class. She dropped her tray in the school cafeteria, and she missed her bus ride home.

WHAT REALLY HAPPENED

By "staying cool" and denying her anger, Elaine avoided dealing with Susan's betrayal and her own fury and embarrassment. But as the day wore on, the block of ice Elaine had used to temporarily freeze her feelings was beginning to melt. By the time she got home, Elaine was so miserable that she took out the anger she was feeling toward Susan on her little sister, and finally herself.

Although she doesn't consciously realize it, Elaine is furious. She's furious with her friend Susan for putting her down in front of the boy she cares about, and she's even angrier because Susan wouldn't let her express these feelings. By saying "I was only kidding," Susan was really saying, "You can't be angry with me. I won't let you." Instead of objecting, Elaine went along with Susan. She tried to push her anger away and to laugh it off.

Now, however, Elaine isn't feeling very good about herself. That's because her anger didn't "just disappear" —it went below the surface, and now she can't even recognize it for what it is. All Elaine knows is that she's feeling something, and that something is pretty awful. How long will Elaine's anger last? That depends upon how complicated it eventually becomes. In an hour she may lose her temper over some "little thing" and take out the rage she's feeling toward Susan on her mother, her cat, or any breakable object in her path. Her parents might then shake their heads and cluck that Elaine has a "terrible temper" and that she really ought to learn "how to control herself" and "how to cool down." But cooling down isn't Elaine's problem. Knowing *when, how,* and *who* to get angry at is. If Elaine had simply expressed her feelings honestly to Susan at the moment when she became the butt of a hostile joke, she wouldn't be so miserable now. But it's not always that easy.

NO SIMPLE SOLUTIONS

Anger is a complicated emotion, and many times it's difficult to know when you are really feeling it. It's even more difficult and frightening to express those feelings. So what do you do? Do you rant and rave and carry on every time someone says something that makes you angry? Sometimes yelling does serve a purpose. But, as you probably know by now, it's not always the best and most effective way to deal with anger. However, neither is quietly sulking and retreating like a wounded puppy. In case no one ever told you, *it's OK to be angry.* There are many ways to say "Listen to me, I'm angry." It's not easy, but you *can* learn more about your own angry feelings and how to express them to other people. Once you begin, you'll feel better. Unlike Elaine, you'll be spending less time feeling miserable and powerless and more time feeling in control of your life and your emotions.

Chapter Two

IT'S MY RIGHT!

Injustice makes everyone angry. "Why me? Nobody else has to!" and "It's not fair!" are things you probably say when you feel you've been treated unfairly. And if that's the case, you have a right to be angry.

Unfortunately, many people are afraid of anger. They imagine that all sorts of horrible things will happen if they express these feelings. So they cleverly disguise anger as something else.

THE BRUSH-OFF

Sometimes saying you're angry, or even feeling it, can be disturbing. But better a little disturbance right away than a big explosion later on.

Returning to the situation between Susan and Elaine, it's obvious that when Susan told Elaine, "Can't you take a joke?" she was really brushing her off. Because, in this case, there was nothing funny about what Susan had done. It was just plain mean, and Elaine wasn't laughing. It was Elaine's right to be angry, and it was Susan's responsibility to deal with that anger. Instead, Susan used the old "Don't make a big deal about it" routine to avoid taking a good look at why she deliberately tried to embarrass her friend. But emotions like anger never just go away. As we saw, Elaine wound up expressing that anger after all. Only, it was at the wrong time and toward the wrong person (herself!).

When was the last time you had a legitimate grievance and you let someone brush you off with one of these familiar phrases:

"Oh, grow up!"
"Be logical."
"Be calm like me."
"You don't look good when you're angry."
"You look cute when you're angry."
"Don't be irrational."
"Can't you take a little joke?"
"Why are you so sensitive?"

These are only a few of the handy expressions people might use to make you feel ashamed, embarrassed, or afraid to express yourself. By saying that you look cute or ugly when you're angry, someone is responding to the way you *look* rather than the way you *feel*. This is a clever way to make you feel self-conscious and to distract you from your real emotions. Being put off or being put down when you're angry doesn't make you feel better and never really resolves an argument. When a friend or relative uses these brush-off tactics, it's important to know why.

SUSAN'S FEARS

If we take a closer look at the situation between Susan and Elaine, a lot of confusing things suddenly become very clear. Susan had done something cruel to her friend and she knew it. She was feeling guilty, and maybe even a little ashamed. She also knew, deep down, that she was wrong. Like most people in a similar situation, Susan had imaginary fears about what would happen if Elaine really had a chance to express her anger. Maybe she thought that if Elaine got angry, she would make a scene, hit her, or stop being her friend. Instead of taking the chance that any of these things might happen, Susan tricked Elaine into pushing her feelings aside. But the truth of the matter is that anger can be *constructive* and *healthy*. It is a form of communication and part of who you are. Like any of your other feelings, anger is an expression of *your* needs, what *you* care about, and the kind of person *you* would like to be.

THE GREAT ESCAPE

No one goes through life without ever feeling angry at someone or something. But, unfortunately, most of us try

to avoid and deny this feeling as much as possible. (
reason is fear. We fear anger because we think it means
we are immature, illogical, or even insane. The ironic
thing about all this is that, in many cases, the methods
we use to avoid anger are far more destructive than the
feelings themselves. For example, alcoholism, drug addiction, overeating (or under eating), nail biting, sexual
promiscuity, practical jokes, and bullying are often con-
venient ways to avoid saying "Listen to me, I'm angry."

For most of us, it's much easier to disappear into a
television program or eat a chocolate cake than to acknowledge that we are angry and that we have a right to be.
These patterns of avoidance are often easier because
they're so familiar, for we learned them when we were
very young. We watch our parents or older brothers and
sisters do some of these things. Then, without really trying,
we are soon doing them ourselves.

HOW IT CAN BEGIN

How your family deals with anger can reveal important
clues about your own response to this emotion. One
teenager, Brenda, explains it this way:

"Whenever I did something to make my mother angry,
she would always scream, 'Wait till your father gets
home!' It was as though he was the only one who was
allowed to show any anger. So after a while I got the
idea that anger was so scary and dangerous that only
men, especially my father, could deal with it. I really
believed that it was 'unfeminine' to get angry. So I tried
to walk around with a big smile on my face all the time.
No matter how I felt, I always tried to look cheerful. I

thought that if I looked happy and smiley, people would like me and like to be around me. But, eventually, it got so that I didn't like myself. I was holding in all my real feelings. Instead of being cheerful and bouncy, I was pretty depressed."

Seventeen-year-old Paul had a similar experience:

"My older brother, Mark, was always pulling fast ones on me. He'd trick me, tease me, or make snide little jokes about me in front of people I cared about. He'd work me up until finally I couldn't hold it in anymore. Then I'd lose control and start shouting and carrying on. At this point, he'd calmly swagger up to me and say, 'Can't you take it like a man?' Mark was trying to teach me that to be a 'real man' I had to be cool and never show any anger. But after a while I found that I was trying to be cool so much that I had turned into a phony. I was afraid that I couldn't feel *anything*."

Like Brenda and Paul, many of us are brought up with the belief that anger is "unladylike," "unmanly," "immature," or even dangerous. Many parents tell their children that they should "be seen and not heard" or that "talking back is disrespectful." The trouble with these attitudes is that they assume that all anger is unreasonable and they don't eliminate the feelings. They simply stop you from expressing them in healthy ways. Accepting these attitudes means that you will feel anger is bad and destructive and fear that people may not like or love you if you honestly say you're angry about something. Now, deep down, where you're hardly aware of it, will be the feeling that you really have no right to be angry about anything. When this happens, everything becomes very confusing. If someone does do something unfair or cruel to you, you won't be able to tell them in an honest way. Many times you probably won't say anything at all. Instead, you will find an easy "out." Running away, cracking a joke, or picking on your little sister (who had nothing to do with it) are some easy outs. Getting depressed, sulking, or even crying hysterically are others. None of these things sound very easy. But, if you really believe that anger is painful and unhealthy, anything else is easy by comparison.

BREAKING THE PATTERNS

Does all this mean that your parents, brothers, sisters, teachers, and friends are wrong and that you have been a helpless victim of their mistakes? Not really. The more you learn about yourself and emotions in general, the more you'll discover that the words "right" and "wrong" don't always apply to feelings. Everyone has reasons for avoiding anger, but that doesn't mean that they must become *your* reasons. In some situations, you might have to be the first to break a destructive pattern of avoiding or denying anger. You may have to express your anger in order to prove it *can* have positive results.

One of the most positive results of expressing anger is that it can actually *improve* your relationships with other people. Since anger is part of who you are, it is dishonest and phony to pretend that "nothing ever bothers you" and that you are cool and calm all the time. In friendships, honesty can make the difference between real loyalty and feelings of mistrust or suspicion.

Have you ever suspected that certain friends were talking behind your back, gossiping about you, or just wouldn't be there when you really needed them? Then you know what lack of trust feels like. Trust and loyalty between friends (and that includes boy friends and girl friends) are not always easy to establish. But these things will never be established if you don't talk honestly about your real feelings.

If we take a closer look at the situation between Susan and Elaine, we can see how a relationship between two people can deteriorate without emotional honesty.

A WILTING FRIENDSHIP

Susan may have been unfair when she made fun of Elaine. But Elaine was unfair too. By not telling Susan what she was really feeling, she put their friendship in danger. Elaine agreed (silently, of course) not to "rock the boat" by getting upset. This satisfied Susan, who was afraid of what might happen if Elaine really did express her anger. Both girls acted as if nothing had happened and everything was just fine.

Only it wasn't. Will this kind of emotional dishonesty hurt their friendship? Yes. Because by pretending that everything between them is settled, they are agreeing not to express their *real* feelings. Without knowing each other's real feelings, they can't really know one another. That's because what you *feel* tells someone a lot about who you *are*.

In this type of situation, many things can happen—none of them good. When people don't talk openly about their feelings, they find other ways to express them. These two friends might betray each other's secrets. They might spread gossip, or simply grow cold and let their friendship fade. And since anger doesn't just disappear, it's more than likely Elaine's fury will come out in one of those sneaky, destructive ways.

Like many of us, Elaine was afraid to express her anger. She felt uncomfortable about sharing her feelings with Susan. She was also afraid that if she did, it would destroy their friendship. But by not telling Susan that she was angry, Elaine really began to destroy the friendship. Eventually this pattern of withholding feelings and then letting them sneak out in other ways will cause problems and confusion. The two girls will discover that they no longer really like or trust each other. The friendship will slowly turn sour. Yet chances are that neither Susan nor Elaine will ever understand why.

FIRST THINGS FIRST

There have probably been times in your life when you've been hurt and angry but thought it best not to "rock the boat" by expressing these emotions. Maybe you really believed and still believe the old maxim that "children should be seen and not heard." Maybe you've been afraid that saying you're angry means screaming it —and no one enjoys losing their temper. It's not easy to tell someone that they have made you angry. It's even more difficult to acknowledge that you really *are* angry.

If you take a close look at your own life, you might discover that you are confused by a lot of your own behavior. Maybe, like Elaine, you eat too much or you eat the wrong things. You might have become the class clown, the class dunce, or the neighborhood bully. It could be that some of this behavior is a result of holding back your real feelings. But you can break this pattern and learn how to tell anyone—even your parents—that you're angry. Only, first, you've got to be able to acknowledge that *it's OK to be angry.* After you've done this, you'll be able to find constructive ways to express your anger.

NOW, THE GOOD NEWS

You might ask, "How do I know when I have a right to be angry, and how do I know when it's best not to express my feelings?" Maybe you're afraid to get in touch with all the anger you feel for one simple reason: you're afraid you'll be shouting and throwing temper tantrums all the time.

Well, the good news is that there is no emotional judge and jury. Angry feelings aren't "right" or "wrong"—they just *are.* You can be angry at a specific incident, or you can just feel angry that you can't have more control over your own life. The important thing is to acknowledge anger as a *legitimate* feeling.

Love and happiness are legitimate feelings. No one expects you to disguise or hold in your happy, loving feelings. Most people are not afraid of a "love tantrum" or a "fit of happiness." That's because most of us have learned to accept love and happiness as part of the feelings that make us human.

But anger is one of those feelings too. Once you realize that anger isn't "bad" or "wrong," you'll realize that it doesn't have to be expressed by screaming or by violence. These things happen when you hold angry feelings in for so long that you finally boil over. When you are afraid of your angry feelings, you can't express them constructively. You might let other people brush you off with "don't rock the boat" attitudes. You might let your angry feelings pile up. But you aren't doing yourself any favors because when you finally reach that boiling point, someone, maybe you, will get burned!

WHERE TO GO FROM HERE

Understanding more about anger and learning why and when you get angry will help you overcome your fear of this emotion. Learning how to express your angry feelings will help you feel better about other people and about yourself. But all this will take some work. It means you might have to drop the "cool" act in order to prevent boiling over later on. It also means that you'll have to take a good look at yourself and spend some time trying to understand who you really are and what you really feel.

Chapter Three

IT'S ONLY A MOLEHILL, SO WHY DOES IT FEEL LIKE A MOUNTAIN?

Sometimes you don't exactly know the cause of your anger. This can lead to confusion, fear, and frustration. Did you ever get the distinct feeling you were furious but weren't sure why? Have you ever flown off the handle at some "little thing" that ordinarily might not get you angry at all? This sort of anger is the type that's difficult to understand and even harder to get under control. That's because it probably doesn't have much to do with the present. It's related to something that happened a long time ago—so long ago you may have almost forgotten about it, but not quite.

DOWN MEMORY LANE

Somewhere inside your brain you have an internal filing cabinet. There you store for future reference just about everything that ever happens to you. Along with all the good memories are the angry ones, too. And these memories go a long way back, all the way to when you were an infant crying and squirming in your crib.

As a matter of fact, that's where you first learned about anger. Babies get angry and frustrated almost as often as they experience happy feelings. As they grow older and have more control over their environment, they have less cause for anger and frustration. But inside everyone's brain there is a place where even these early angers are stored and recorded. Since it would be impossible to be constantly aware of *all* these events, part of the mind simply files them away under "old memories." But sometimes a little molehill of an incident happens to touch one of those ancient, nearly forgotten angers. Although you may not be immediately aware of what's going on, when one of those old angers is rekindled—watch out!

Most of the time it's not easy to trace an angry feeling back through your memory file. If you get furious at some little incident, it's hard to figure out what really triggered your extreme reaction. One reason is that you are wrapped up in the anger. Another reason is that you may not realize your present anger is really connected to something that occurred a long time ago. When this happens, you might have to climb up that mountain of anger in order to gain a better view of how you got there. In other words, you'll have to review each incident and try to figure out what made you so angry. Then, when you're calmer, you should take a good look inside yourself. There's usually an old familiar reason for what you're feeling. But you may need some help finding it.

BILL'S SEARCH

For Bill, "making mountains out of molehills" was an old story. He'd get angry at some little thing, yell and carry on, but never really understand why he was so furious. Yelling didn't make him feel any better either. That's because he sensed he was missing something. He knew that what he was yelling about wasn't the only cause for his anger, but he couldn't figure out what was until he learned how to trace his path up the mountain of his own feelings. Here's Bill's description of his journey:

"I guess this has happened to everyone at some time or another. I was sitting in Mr. Sloan's math class. Everyone was talking, but of course he caught me. He told me I had to stay after school for ten minutes. Sure, I was talking, but so was everyone else. I just had the bad luck to get caught. The punishment was no big deal. I had nothing to do after school anyway. But I felt myself get that horrible angry feeling. Then I felt miserable. It seemed like the whole world was picking on me and that it would always be that way. Everything in my life suddenly seemed hopeless.

"Then I began to imagine getting even with Mr. Sloan—sort of a revenge for his picking on me. I thought of how it would be if *I* were the teacher and *he* had to stay after school. I imagined how powerful I would be, and how all my friends would gang up on him and make *him* miserable.

Right after that, I began to let my mind drift to fantasies about running away. All of a sudden, I saw myself getting on a plane and heading for some faraway, exotic place. When everyone discovered that I was gone, they'd all be sorry. Especially Mr. Sloan!

"But obviously none of these fantasies really made much sense. As soon as they were over, I was feeling worse than before. After school I stayed ten minutes, staring at the blackboard and watching the clock. When my time was up, I went to my sister Sheila's house. She has a couple of kids, and fooling around with them usually cheers me up. This time it didn't. As soon as I got there, I walked into the kitchen table and knocked over a gallon of milk. What a mess! I began screaming at the kitchen table, my little nephew, my sister, Mr. Sloan, and the whole world! I know this sounds silly, but it really felt like I was being punished all over again."

When Bill arrived at his sister's house, he was still angry and upset at what had happened in class. It's pretty unusual to go through school and never get into a situation similar to Bill's. It's happened to most of us. Only, to Bill, it meant a lot more than simply being punished for talking. It had something to do with an old anger that had never been resolved. But with his sister's help, Bill was able to understand his feelings. Here's how:

"When Sheila walked into the kitchen and saw the mess, she knew I was in trouble. She helped me clean it up and we sat down to talk. I told her what had happened and how unfair the whole world was. We discussed the incident and I agreed that I was talking in class. In reality, the punishment was no big thing. As a matter of fact, the whole incident was nothing to get very angry about.

"Then Sheila asked me if this had happened before. It had, but not with Mr. Sloan. About four months earlier, in health class, four other kids and I were caught passing notes. We had had to stay after school and I remembered that I was pretty angry then, too. Sheila asked me who else, besides Mr. Sloan and my health teacher, did I feel picked on me or singled me out. At first I couldn't think of anyone. But something about that feeling was strangely familiar. It didn't hit me immediately, but as I sat there I tried to pinpoint when I had first experienced this feeling. Then I realized that it was at home.

"I had always felt that my father had singled me out because I was the youngest. But I never tried to talk to him about it. Instead, when he picked on me, I usually ran to my room and slammed the door. I was always afraid to tell him how angry and helpless he made me feel. So when Mr. Sloan singled me out, it reminded me of my father. All the anger I'd never expressed to Dad came out at Mr. Sloan, the kitchen table, and my little nephew.

"After my talk with Sheila, I felt better. I was afraid I was going crazy because I had gotten so steamed up at such a little thing. But once I saw what the cause of my anger really was, at least I understood what was happening to me. It made me feel a lot better!"

OPENING THE FLOODGATES

Like Bill, you have probably had times when you've felt you were experiencing too much anger too soon. And even after you expressed that rage, you didn't feel any better. When this happens, you are probably touching on an old anger. Bill's punishment in class wasn't what made him so furious. But it was a reminder of an old problem that had been a source of anger for a long time. The old problem was painful to deal with, so Bill had filed away his anger. He had tried to forget that his father had often made him feel singled out, helpless, and picked on. Bill couldn't really forget these feelings. He could only push them deeper beneath the surface. Later, when Mr. Sloan made him feel the same way, the old feelings about his father were reactivated. All the anger that Bill was sure he had safely filed away under "old memories" rushed out when he least expected it.

Since Mr. Sloan and Bill's father were both older men and authority figures, it was easy for Bill to transfer the anger he had felt toward his father onto his teacher. Only, it wasn't so easy for Bill to figure out what he was doing. It took hard work. It was difficult for Bill to see the similarities between this classroom situation and the one at home.

SIGNPOSTS FOR IRRATIONAL ANGER

Bill became frightened because he thought he was "going crazy." But, of course, he wasn't. He was just experiencing something called "irrational anger." This is an anger that doesn't appear to make any rational sense. But, as we've already discussed, feelings may not always be "right" or "wrong"—they may or may not seem to make sense—they just *are*. Nevertheless, it's important to accept and come to terms with all your feelings, whether they seem to make sense or not. That's because each feeling you have is a very important part of who you are. Searching through your memory file isn't as easy as looking through a real filing cabinet. It means looking back and looking inward in order to solve the mystery of your own very special feelings. When you feel irrational anger you might, like Bill, be afraid you're crazy or you may just get very confused. There *are* ways to deal with this kind of "sneaky" anger. It is possible to get to the bottom of the mystery. But first you'll have to know how to identify irrational anger.

Clue #1—You Hate the World

This is the first clue to knowing if your anger is irrational. You feel anger not only at someone or something in particular—but at the whole world. You may also realize that the intensity of your rage is far out of proportion to the situation. Then you may find yourself asking, "Why am I feeling so angry?"

Clue #2—You Can't Let Go

The worst thing about irrational anger is that you can't "shake it" because you don't know what causes it. Taking revenge, slamming doors, calling someone names, and even punishing yourself just don't seem to help. You're still angry and it doesn't make sense that you are. If this is true, it's a good bet that you're experiencing irrational anger.

Clue #3—You Let Your Anger Spread

You take the anger you felt at a particular person or situation and let it spread to other people, or even to inanimate objects. Bill did this when he "accidentally" spilled the milk. Then he let his anger spread to the table (now, that really *is* irrational), which he yelled at, and finally to his nephew and his sister. Because he didn't really know why he was angry in the first place, Bill had no way to resolve his feelings. He kept getting angrier and angrier and striking out at whatever was in front of him.

Clue #4—You Feel Confused

Since irrational anger doesn't make immediate sense, when you feel this way your behavior won't seem logical to you either. Bill daydreamed about taking revenge on Mr. Sloan and about running away. You may want to hit someone, break something, or become someone else. Sometimes these irrational thoughts can be scary. You can be frightened into thinking that maybe you really are "losing your mind." But you're not. You're just stumbling around in a very dark room and you need to find the light. The dark room is your anger. Finding the light means finding the real cause for your intense feelings.

LOCATING THE SWITCH

There really is a light in that dark room. You don't have to be afraid of your irrational anger because there are ways to trace it back to your memory file. And it's

ways there. Irrational anger doesn't come out of no-
..here. Sometimes you, like Bill, may need outside help.
But you can also help yourself. The next time you feel
irrational anger, ask yourself these questions. Give yourself plenty of time to think about the answers.

- Is my anger irrational? (Check back for the four clues.)
- When was the last time I felt like this?
- At what exact moment did I begin to feel so angry?
- What does this situation remind me of?
- Who does the person I'm angry at remind me of?
- If I weren't feeling so angry, what other feelings (hurt, helplessness, fear, disappointment, and the like) could I allow myself to feel?

Many times it may be too difficult for you to figure out
what's causing your anger. One reason may be that the
real cause is too painful to remember. You may have
walled up that old anger so well that you're unable to
connect it to the present situation. When this happens, it's
best to ask someone you trust for help. Friends can
ask you questions that can gently guide you back to
your old buried anger. They can reassure you that you
aren't crazy, and that they have felt irrational anger too.
Their feelings may give you some clues about your own
feelings. When you have found the cause of your anger,
you'll know. You will feel better. Your confusion will be
cleared up, and you will have learned a lot more about
yourself.

Sometimes an old memory is so deeply buried that, even
with the help of a friend, you just can't unearth it. If
this happens, you can still do some positive things. First,

acknowledge that you were feeling angry (that's OK, remember?). Second, be aware that your anger was irrational. Third, you can relax and feel better just knowing that the anger was connected to something that happened a long time ago and that you weren't crazy for overreacting.

Then you can make an effort to keep this anger in your "active memory file." You can write about it in a journal or a diary. Describe the incident as completely as possible. What got you angry? Who got you angry? What were your exact feelings? Try to find a central theme to your feelings.

For example, Bill felt he was being picked on. You may feel people are laughing at you, putting you down, or ignoring you completely. Sometimes looking for a common theme to your angry feelings may help you discover a whole chain of old memories. The chances are that some future incident will reactivate that old anger again. Only, this time, you'll have a lot more information to use in tracking down the real cause. The feeling will be more familiar and less confusing. When you keep an "active memory file," you'll eventually be able to understand and to deal with more of your feelings.

Chapter Four

RED HOT AND READY TO FIGHT!

How did you ever get into this? Your face is burning, your hands are trembling, you're moving at a pace that seems faster than the speed of light. You feel as if you're going to explode.

But relax—balloons burst, people don't! A hot temper can be frightening, but it's not the only way to express anger. It's just *one* way. As you've seen, anger never really disappears. You can push it back into your memory file, or you can let it out. But sometimes *how* you let it out can become a problem in itself.

No one likes losing his or her temper. One reason is the horrible feeling that you are out of control. Being out of control of your own feelings is like being the pilot of an airplane that's headed for a collision. You know disaster is unavoidable, but it's too late to bail out. Like most airplane crashes, temper tantrums almost always end in disaster. In other words, losing your temper isn't just uncomfortable, embarrassing, and scary, it also rarely gets you what you want. How can you avoid being taken for a ride by your temper? Well, the first step is trying to understand just what it is that causes such outbursts of anger.

A STORAGE PROBLEM

The problem with storing up old angers usually arises when you run out of space. The angers you have ignored, pushed away, and buried eventually pile up. Soon there just doesn't seem to be any more room in your head for all your feelings. When this happens, something has to be released in order to make room for other emotions. If you can't let your stored anger out in a logical, sensible way, it just might burst out in a wild, uncontrolled manner. Screaming, throwing things, punching, gnashing your teeth, crying, and slamming doors are all examples of what happens when buried angers burst out from your memory file.

This explosive display of angry fireworks is often compared to a pressure cooker. As water gets hot, the temperature rises. Eventually, there is a release of steam. As a matter of fact, one way we describe losing our temper is actually called "letting off steam." But the difference between a pressure cooker and your feelings is obvious. Unlike steam released by a pressure cooker, emotional steam is nearly always destructive. Also, a fit of temper usually doesn't solve anything. It doesn't make you feel better, and, most important, it doesn't resolve the problem that caused the angry feelings in the first place.

NO LONG-TERM BENEFIT

"Letting off steam" and having a "good yell" or a "good cry" are only temporary solutions. When you do these things you are really only putting out one tiny spark. The big internal bonfire of anger you have trapped inside keeps right on burning. That's why people who are troubled with "bad tempers" can't seem to overcome their problem. They hold things in until the pressure becomes unbearable. Then the show begins. There's a lot of loud, threatening, and even destructive behavior. But after they have calmed down, it's only a matter of time (days, weeks, or months) until a wave of temper carries them helplessly away again.

The reason for this is not difficult to understand. Fits of temper only *express* anger. They do not *resolve* angry feelings. The best way to stop feeling angry is not by acting angry, but by trying to understand more about your angry feelings. If you try to take a good, honest look at your feelings, you won't have to bury them deep inside yourself. Then you'll be free to experience other emotions. So although "letting off steam" may have a temporary cooling effect, it doesn't really put out the fire.

FEELING VERSUS ACTING

But what can you do when you really get out of control? Like the times when someone says or does something and all of a sudden you feel that old scary feeling building up inside again. For some people, that feeling is marked by a pounding heart. Other people experience intense headaches, begin to sweat, and really do "see red." These are physical clues that an explosion of anger is on the way.

If you have a problem temper, you have probably experienced anger as a physical sensation. When there is an emotional conflict going on inside, it's not unusual for your body to react to that conflict. In this case, one part of you is desperately trying to push the anger back down into your memory file, while another part of you is trying to push the anger out. When, and if, the anger does burst out, the result is a moment of blind fury—a moment in which you may say and do things you might regret later on. But "letting it all out" isn't the only way to release your anger. You can cool off and express your anger without hurting someone else or embarrassing yourself. In order to do this, you'll have to understand one very important thing. There is a difference between *feeling* angry and *acting* angry.

HELEN'S TESTY TEMPER

Helen is one of those people who worries about her "problem temper." She often finds herself in situations when she feels out of control and carried away by feelings of rage. When this happens, she gets into trouble with her parents, teachers, and friends. Helen's temper eventually became a major problem. She found herself having to stay home on weekends, missing out on special school trips, and losing friends because of her constant outbursts. Here's Helen's description of one of her typical temper outbursts:

"This time I really made up my mind that no matter what happened, I would *not* lose my temper. I was tired of always getting into trouble because of what I said or did when I got angry. Also, I was scared of losing control. It's frightening when I'm carried away by my feelings. But, as usual, when something gets me angry, I wind up having a real blowout.

"For example, last week my mother told me I would have to baby-sit for my little sister on Friday night. She had to visit my grandmother in the hospital and our regular sitter was busy. That just *happened* to be the night of the big basketball game. When she told me, I got very angry. I just couldn't control myself. I started screaming and calling my mother all sorts of names. I reminded her of all the times she had treated me like this. I told her she was a bad mother and a selfish person. Then I got really furious. I went into the bathroom and smashed her favorite bottle of perfume. Of course, I was then punished for the next weekend as well. I know that I only made it tougher on myself by doing what I did. But I was just so angry I felt I had no choice."

When we take a close look at what happened to Helen, we can begin to understand the difference between *feeling* angry and *acting* angry. Being told she had to baby-sit on the night of the big game made Helen very angry. It was perfectly OK for Helen to feel angry. Who wouldn't be upset about missing something they had been looking forward to? But Helen's angry feelings did not have to result in a temper tantrum. She could have expressed those same feelings in a very different way. Her angry behavior (the temper tantrum) was destructive. She insulted her mother and broke something. This prevented her from going out the next weekend as well.

Helen didn't realize the difference between angry *feelings* and angry *actions*. She *did* have a choice. She could have expressed her angry feelings in a way that would not have been destructive—in a manner that might even have helped her to achieve her goal (not baby-sitting for her little sister). Helen worries about her temper. She is afraid that she can't stop her angry feelings from hurting someone else. But angry feelings are part of life. They tell you something about who you are and what is important to you. Angry, destructive actions do not have to be the result of those feelings. One good way to avoid losing yourself to your temper is to create a "safety zone" between what you *feel* inside and what you *do*.

TIME OUT

The safety zone is a period of time *you* create. It can be a few minutes, or even a few hours, between the time you first *feel* angry and the time you *do* something about those feelings. For example, Helen could have taken a few moments between the time when her mother informed her that she had to baby-sit and the time when she began to scream and break things. Retreating into your safety zone can help you avoid senseless, frightening, and destructive fury. During this time, you give yourself room to feel safe and to explore the causes of the conflict, what you're feeling, and what (if anything) you can do about it. It does take a little control. But if you stop and pull back from a heated situation, you might be able to deal with it in a more sensible way. This really can help you avoid the endless cycle of losing your temper, cooling off, and then losing your temper again.

Suppose that, after Helen's mother told her the bad news, Helen had stopped to think things through. The situation might have gone this way:

Helen could have told herself, "Boy, am I angry. It really is unfair to let me know about this hospital visit at the last minute. Of course, I hadn't told her about the game either. But unless I think of a way out of this one, I'll be stuck home all night. Maybe I can think of someone else who can sit tonight. Now let's see . . ."

In this situation, Helen would have admitted she was angry but decided not to let her feelings result in destructive behavior. If she had been able to find someone else to sit, she could have gone to the game that night. But if not, she might have been able to work out a compromise plan with her mother. Maybe her mother would have agreed to giving her some extra privileges in the future as payment for helping out on such short notice. She also might have reached an agreement in which her mother would come home early and she would have had to miss only part of the game. Any of these things would have been more constructive than what did happen. If you, like Helen, find that you just seem to "fly off the handle" too quickly, you might need some help getting into your safety zone so you can work things out in a sensible, constructive way.

One way to retreat into your safety zone is to count to ten. Another way is to go someplace where you can be alone and wait, until you can think clearly. But if these methods don't work for you, there are others that will.

If you can hold back your anger long enough to grab a pencil, why not write yourself into your safety zone? Simply write down on paper exactly what you're feeling. Don't leave anything out. Every thought and feeling is important. You should even include all the different things you wish you could do to "get even" or "get out" of the situation.

Then separate all the thoughts and feelings into two groups. One group should contain the ideas that make sense and are possible. The other group should list all the ideas that are destructive to your goal, or that are simply impossible or illogical.

If the list that makes sense is small, or doesn't exist at all, try to think of some logical, constructive things you *can* do. Think of ways that you can make your anger work *for* you. This includes thinking of ways to negotiate with someone else. A good negotiation always involves some sort of compromise. To reach a satisfactory compromise, you might have to give up something that is not very important in order to gain something that is. For example, Helen might have been able to get some extra privileges because she helped her mother when she was needed. First, decide what your immediate goal is. (Helen's was going to the basketball game.)

If you are involved in a power struggle with someone else, decide what you want to win. Then figure out what you'd settle for. Sometimes the only constructive thing you can think of may just be to stay in your safety zone a little longer. You may also decide to wait a day or two and then talk it over with the person you're angry with.

If you can't take the time to write things down, or if you just don't like that idea, try walking away from your temper. Remove yourself from a "hot" situation and take a long walk. As you walk, try talking to yourself (out loud or silently). Express *all* your feelings—even the most frightening ones. This is the time to yell if you feel like it. Make the two lists of possible and impossible solutions in your head. Eliminate all the senseless, destructive solutions. Then concentrate on ideas that can help you achieve your goals.

This walking time is valuable. It can help release the physical energy that is part of your emotional buildup. You might feel exhausted after a short walk when you are very angry. But the chances are that you'll have prevented yourself from acting destructively.

If writing or walking isn't your style, maybe talking is. You can talk about these same angry feelings by using a tape recorder. Talking into a tape recorder is like having a telephone conversation with yourself. Later you can play the tape back. Then you can decide what your ideas and feelings were really all about. After you've had a chance to hear yourself out, give yourself the time you need to develop a constructive way to express your angry feelings.

You can also call a friend and discuss your feelings with him or her. This type of "buddy system" can help you get into your safety zone. Once there, you'll be able to sort out your feelings and choose a more constructive method of dealing with them. And by listening to your friends as they discuss their angry feelings, you can also learn a lot more about your own. Sometimes just knowing that you're not the only one in the world with an explosive temper can make you feel a lot better. Walking, talking, and writing are just three ways that you can get into your safety zone. However, since everyone is different, you may discover another method that works for you. You might even want to talk about your feelings one time and write about them the next. Anything that helps you build a safety zone between your feelings and your behavior will help prevent temper outbursts. But there is a difference between using your safety zone to cool down and using it as an escape. These activities should give you time to think about your feelings—they should not make you forget them!

Remember, however, that the safety zone method takes time. It might not work all at once. It might work at some times and not at others. Keep trying. The more you try to understand your own feelings, the less you'll feel out of control and afraid. Just keep in mind that while *it's OK to be angry*, your anger doesn't always have to be expressed by a wild explosion of temper.

Chapter Five

THE ANGER YOU DIDN'T KNOW YOU HAD

You know the feeling. You want to eat, drink, ride in a fast car, cry, and bite your nails all at the same time. You're feeling a lot of things, but anger just isn't one of them—or is it?

Anger isn't always obvious. But at least when you're slamming doors, screaming, and getting red in the face, you're expressing hostile feelings often associated with anger. You may not like the feelings. You may not know what's causing them. But you do know, without a doubt, that you're furious. Sometimes, however, you can be just as furious and not show it, at least not in the usual way.

And sometimes this means that you have really sealed the lid on your anger.

Have you ever felt depressed, guilty, anxious, hungry, or tired and not known exactly why? These feelings are sometimes cover-ups for something else. Behind the boredom, the depression, the guilt, and the hunger there's another feeling. Many times that feeling is anger. But why would you want to cover up your anger with anything as awful as depression, guilt, or boredom? Why do some people overeat, take drugs, get drunk, or get sick rather than get angry? The answers aren't simple. They are complex and different for every individual.

THE GREAT PRETENDERS

A cover-up is a disguise. Like most disguises, cover-ups, especially emotional cover-ups, are used to hide what you're really feeling. If we go back to the pressure cooker image, it might be easier to understand why anger sometimes takes such strange forms. When your rage begins to build, like the temperature of liquid inside a pressure cooker, it must eventually be released. One way to release that fury is to let it out in a quick, explosive burst. This is what happens when you lose your temper.

But everyone doesn't let his or her anger out this way, and some people only use this type of release some of the time. What other ways are there to express anger? Plenty. But the most common one is to *turn the anger inward, against yourself*. When this happens, you take the anger you feel toward other people or situations and redirect it so that you harm yourself.

The problem with turning anger inward is that you can do some pretty destructive things to yourself and not know why. The reason you do these things is because you don't want to feel the anger or you're afraid to feel the anger. So you use another emotion to conceal what you're really feeling.

People who claim they're "never angry," "never lose their temper," and are "easygoing" all the time are probably not aware of their own emotional cover-ups. Everyone gets angry sometimes. Most of us get angry a lot. Relax. These feelings are normal. Running away or hiding your feelings can lead to trouble. Denying that you ever get angry is one clue that you probably are guilty of the "big cover-up." Somewhere inside you, beneath all those other emotions, you've probably buried a rage that you've never expressed in a way you can understand and cope with.

MERRY, MISERABLE MADELINE

Madeline is one of those people who "never gets angry." As a matter of fact, Madeline is the typical "fat and jolly" teenager. However, everyone knows that being fat is nothing to be jolly about. So why is Madeline laughing and smiling so much? Here's how she explains it:

"I know I overeat. But I just can't seem to help myself. Both my parents work, and I have four little brothers. When I get home from school, they're all there waiting for me. Each one wants something else. But no one ever asks me what *I* want. I guess I have a lot of responsibility. Sometimes eating just makes me feel better. It gives me this safe feeling inside. But the funny thing is, I never feel satisfied. I just keep stuffing myself like a pig. I hate the way I look, and sometimes I hate myself for eating so much. I've tried diets, but they don't work. I just can't stop eating."

Madeline has turned the anger she feels toward other people inward against herself. It's possible that Madeline needs to feel safe. She might also have other needs. It makes her angry that her needs aren't being met by her parents, her brothers, or any other people in her life.

But she never tells anyone what she is feeling or discharges her anger in a way that might give them a hint about how she feels. Instead, she has devised a way to "stuff the anger down inside herself." When she eats and eats, she is doing just that. Afterward Madeline doesn't feel any better. In fact, she hates herself. But, for Madeline, it's easier to direct this hatred and anger toward herself than toward her brothers or her parents or her friends. One reason why Madeline never feels satisfied after eating is that she has betrayed her real feelings. She's afraid to tell the people in her life what she really needs and how angry she feels. Instead, she has chosen (and this *is* a choice) to hurt herself by becoming fat and unattractive. It's possible that Madeline isn't the "happy fat girl" after all. Underneath all those smiles and all that extra weight is a person who is very unhappy and *very angry*.

PETER'S RETREAT

Depression is a sad feeling that seems to come from nowhere. Sometimes a gray rainy day or a sad movie or book might make you feel depressed. But if you feel depressed a lot of the time and don't know why, you are probably guilty of a cover-up. Depression is a way to punish yourself. Feeling depressed most of the time can prevent you from enjoying life.

For some people weeks, and even months, can go by when it might as well be raining every day. That's because inside themselves everything is gray and sad. Although on the outside these people may have pretty satisfying lives, they won't allow themselves to enjoy them.

Peter is one of these people. He feels depressed a lot. Sometimes he doesn't go to school, visit friends, or even leave his room. Here's how he describes his feelings:

"I just feel depressed all the time. I don't know when this started. But I know I didn't always feel this blue. When we lived in Philadelphia, I had lots of friends, belonged to the hockey team, and was a pretty active guy. But since we moved to Colorado, nothing seems to be the same. I have my own room and go to a nice school. My dad has a real important job, but we don't play ball together like we used to. Some of my friends from the old neighborhood stopped writing. I guess I'm just depressed about all this."

On the surface Peter is depressed. And deep down he's also angry. He's angry that he had to move, that his father doesn't spend as much time with him as he used to, and that his friends no longer keep in touch with him. Peter could tell his father that he misses the times they had shared and that it makes him angry to be neglected. He could write to his friends and explain how important their letters are to him. But, for Peter, it's easier to cop out and withdraw into a depression.

Peter is punishing himself for feeling angry. Instead

of expressing his anger toward his father or his friends, he has turned it against himself in the form of depression. Peter probably believes that he doesn't have the right to these angry feelings. Unfortunately, as long as Peter feels this way and continues to cover-up, his life will be one long series of gray rainy days. Wouldn't it just be easier to get in touch with that anger and to express it in a constructive way rather than cover it up with depression?

ANGER, THE DANGEROUS FUEL

Depression and overeating are two common cover-ups, but there are many more. "Acting out of anger" is another frequent and very destructive cover-up. For most of us, it is easier to do angry things than it is to get in touch with those feelings and to do something constructive to resolve them. What does acting out of anger mean in real life?

Let's take a look at two teenagers, Valerie and Danny. Both of them deny that they ever feel angry, but both are acting out of anger most of the time. Danny is an alcoholic, and Valerie is pregnant. Neither one is very happy about the state they are in. But they have no idea how they helped to get themselves there or how they can change their lives. Danny explains it this way:

"I like to drink. I don't know what else to say. It started with beer when I was fourteen. Now, two years later, I drink anything I can get my hands on. Sometimes I get so drunk I black out. Once I took my brother's car and nearly totaled it. My parents want me to get help. They can't understand why I'm like this. They are always talking about how well my brother turned out, and what an 'A' student he always was. He's so high and mighty that I can't even talk to him. I guess I'm just no good."

Valerie, eight months pregnant at seventeen, also thinks she's inferior:

"I started to have a 'bad reputation' in the seventh grade. You see, I always knew that I wasn't pretty or smart or anything. I'm nothing like my older sister, Jo Ann. She always had lots of dates. I wanted to have boy friends too. My friends always talk about how popular and pretty Jo Ann is. But Jo Ann never really helped me or gave me advice. Instead, she'd make fun of my skin, my figure, just about everything about me. She didn't even want me around when her dates came to the house. I guess I figured there was only one way a girl like me could have a boy friend. I thought that if I got sexually involved, the boy would learn to love me later on. For a while, even Jo Ann was impressed with my popularity. But now everybody knows why I had so many dates. I'm not angry, really, I'm just unlucky."

At first glance, you might dismiss people like Danny and Valerie as "mixed up" or "immoral." But if you take a second look, you will find that they are really more complicated than that. You might also find some similarities between their behavior and your own. Both Danny and Valerie are acting out of their anger and hurting themselves rather than confronting the people who are causing their rage. They have buried their anger so well that neither one even acknowledges that they *are* angry.

One of the causes for Danny's drinking might be the fact that he is constantly compared to his older brother. He needs and loves his brother, and he is angry about being put down and rejected. Danny is afraid to risk exposing his angry feelings. So the anger that is meant for his brother and other people who compare him to his brother is redirected toward himself. When this happens, the anger takes a different form—alcoholism. Danny's drinking is an expression of his rage. But no one, not even Danny himself, understands why he would rather drink than deal with his deep-rooted anger.

Valerie is in a similar position. She has come to believe that she isn't really worth being loved for who she is. As a result, she is letting herself be used sexually. Instead of standing up to her older sister and saying that she won't tolerate being put down, she has redirected the anger inward, toward herself.

Being an alcoholic, a promiscuous male or female, a drug addict, or a criminal is not fun. People who have experienced any of these things have experienced pain, rejection, frustration, and humiliation. They have also engaged in a big cover-up. By numbing themselves with drugs, liquor, sex, or danger, they hoped to bury their true feelings. Acting out of anger is not the same as acting *on* your anger in a way that will help you achieve your goals and resolve your feelings. Neither Valerie nor Danny nor others like them ever get to the *cause* of their behavior. Unfortunately, until they expose their buried, angry feelings, they will be helplessly caught up in their own cycle of self-destruction. The only way to stop acting out of anger is to get to the bottom of who and what are responsible for these feelings of hopelessness and rage.

WHEN ANGER MAKES YOU SICK

Many people would rather get sick than deal with their anger. "I don't feel good," "My stomach hurts," and "I have a bad pain" can often be cover-ups for feelings that are too frightening to express for what they really are. Getting sick from anger is a common and often misunderstood way of turning the anger you feel toward other people or situations inward against yourself. Many times the illness itself becomes a symbolic expression of that anger. Are people who get sick all the time really sick? Are they hypochondriacs (people who feel, and look, sick but whose illness has psychological rather than physical origins), or are they just angry? The answer can be all three. But whether the illness is psychological or physical in origin, it is still very real and needs medical care and attention. Let's take a look at two teenagers who use illness as a way to express their angry feelings.

Janet says, "I am thirteen and I have an ulcer. I know that sounds awful. Lots of people are surprised when they hear that I have such a serious illness. For a long time no one believed me when I complained—especially my mother. Whenever I told her I couldn't go to school because I had a bad stomachache, she called me a 'chronic complainer' and a 'hypochondriac.' She had a big, important job in an insurance company, and she resented having to stay home to take care of me whenever I said I was sick. I'm a big girl and I don't mind staying home alone. I told her that. But she hired someone to stay with me anyway. Well, after the doctor found the ulcer, she felt terrible that she had never taken me seriously."

Donald says, "I'm seventeen and I've always been healthy. This year I developed asthma. I started getting these attacks that made me feel like I was suffocating. The first time I remember it happening was when I was with my girl friend, Linda. We've been going together for almost two years. But lately she's been talking about getting engaged. I love Linda, but I have big plans for college and travel. I want to stay single until I'm at least twenty-five. But Linda has this thing about getting engaged in our senior year. She even started talking to my mother about it. Now all I hear at home is, 'Linda is such a nice girl. Why don't you think about getting serious? Someone will take her away if you're not careful.' Well, before I knew it, I began to have trouble breathing. When things got really bad, I went to the doctor. He found out I have asthma. What a drag! I hate being sick all the time."

Both Janet and Donald are "really sick," there's no doubt about that. But there is something more to their illness than can be treated by their medical doctors. Their symptoms are also related to their *feelings*. Janet harbors some buried anger about her mother going off to work and not taking her seriously. Developing an ulcer is one way that Janet can get her mother's attention. It is also Janet's way of covering up her anger and turning it against herself. In this case, Janet's anger actually "turns her stomach."

It's also obvious that Donald feels pressured by his girl friend. She is pushing him to make a commitment he isn't ready for. At home the pressure continues. Donald is furious, but he probably believes that it is wrong to get angry at people he loves. His anger is literally "suffocating him." The asthma is real, all right, but it is also a reflection of a rage that he has turned inward. How can you tell if an illness is a result of anger? It can't be emphasized enough that all illnesses should be taken seriously. Even if you do suspect that your problem may be "nerves" or "imagination" or "all in your head," that doesn't mean that it will go away if you ignore it. If you don't feel well, you should always check with your doctor and rule out the possibility of a physical problem. After you've done this, and your doctor tells you he can find nothing physically wrong, you might be guilty of covering up and turning your anger inward. However, as in Janet's and Donald's cases, anger turned inward can also cause physical problems that must be treated medically. But because the true origin is emotional they must also uncover and come to terms with their anger in order to get completely well.

Here are some examples of illnesses that make angry statements:

Stomachaches or ulcers—The anger is "turning my stomach."

Asthma—My anger is "smothering me."

Loss of appetite—I can no longer "swallow my anger."

Constipation—I can't "let go" of my anger.

Vomiting and/or diarrhea—I want to "expel" my angry feelings.

Headaches—It is a pain to "think about" my anger.

Skin rashes, hives, and some allergies—I'm so angry, it shows no matter how I try to hide it.

Remember that illnesses related to feelings are "real" and need to be treated medically. If you have checked with your doctor and no "cause" for an illness can be found, your problem may be emotional. Whether your illness is physical or psychological in origin, you can help yourself by understanding the relationship between your emotional condition and your physical condition.

MORE DETECTIVE WORK

What can you do about self-destructive behavior or illness that you suspect is related to your emotions? You can begin to help yourself by thinking about, and answering, these questions:

- When did I begin this behavior (feeling sick or acting out of anger)?
- What events might have brought on the behavior or illness?
- What might I possibly have to "gain" by being sick or acting out of anger?
- Is there anything that being sick might be helping me to avoid?
- Why might I be afraid to express my anger?
- Am I using myself as a weapon against parents, teachers, or friends? Might I be trying to gain a victory over them through my own defeat?
- If I weren't sick or acting this way, what else might I be feeling?
- Besides being sick, or acting out, what other alternatives do I have?
- How can I stop turning this anger against myself, express it, and make it work for me?

Getting to the bottom of your deep-rooted feelings isn't always easy. These questions may help you begin to think about your problem in a different way. But if you suspect that there is something more to your self-destructive behavior and you can't figure out exactly what, you'll need some outside help. You don't have to be "crazy" or "sick"

to see a counselor, social worker, psychiatrist, psychoanalyst, or psychologist. In many cases, these people can
help you to understand yourself better than anyone else
(and that includes sympathetic friends). Therapy is a
process that can help you to understand yourself and
other people. Wanting to improve your life and your
relationships with others is the main reason for seeking a
therapist. It has nothing at all to do with being "crazy."
As a matter of fact, recognizing that you could use help
figuring things out is a sign of mental health rather than
illness. For more information about therapy and therapists
see chapter 9.

Chapter Six

ANGRY FANTASIES

We all have a fantasy world inside our heads. Whether you call it your imagination, or your "unconscious" or "subconscious" doesn't really make a difference. It's a wonderful place to avenge all your angers. But don't kid yourself—it's not for real.

Although many of your fantasies may seem true-to-life, they are only thoughts and reflections that belong to your inner world. That world is a very special place. It's a place where you can be anyone or anything you want to be, and where you can be all-powerful and all-knowing.

There are no rules in your fantasy world. Gravity doesn't exist, and you can fly like a bird or fall without hitting bottom. Although many of your fantasies may seem "crazy" or "weird," they do have some meaning. That's because there's more to fantasies than flying people and talking animals. Those movies that run inside your head have a very important purpose. They can help you recognize, deal with, and even solve problems.

THROUGH THE RABBIT HOLE

Where do you go when you drift off, or when you stare out of a window and aren't really looking at anything? Most of the time you're taking a short trip into your own inner world.

Daydreaming is one way of imagining or wishing for situations that you know will never come true. But sometimes you might need to travel to another time or another place in order to discharge feelings you find difficult to express in the real world. When someone or something makes you very angry and you can't do anything about it in real life, you can drift off to a place where you *can* do something. In this imaginary world you can avenge your enemies and feel at peace with yourself.

Many times your daydreams may seem violent and even frightening. If you daydream of shooting someone you dislike, it doesn't mean you're "bad" or "brutal." We all have destructive feelings. Your fantasy world is the best place to express these feelings. It's comforting to know that somewhere there is an outlet for secret wishes you might be afraid to express to anyone. But if you simply dismiss your fantasy world as a "nice place to visit every once in a while," you might be missing a very important message. What you fantasize about can give you a big clue toward understanding more about yourself and what you're really feeling.

FACT VERSUS FICTION

Tammie is a twelve-year-old girl who had a quick, fleeting image of something that frightened her. Here's how she describes it:

"I had been having a terrible time with my friend, Marilyn. We had been good pals, and then one day she started avoiding me, talking about me, and giving me dirty looks. After she started acting like this, I was sitting in math class one day just staring out of the window when I fantasized that I pushed Marilyn off a cliff. I mean, I actually felt myself push her and I saw her fall. At first I thought it was pretty funny. It made me feel good. I was so angry at her that I didn't even scream or go for help as I saw her fall. A few days later I found out that Marilyn had been told a terrible lie about me. She thought that I was planning to steal her boy friend. She had been reacting to a rumor that she thought was true.

"When we finally cleared up the misunderstanding, we became good friends again. But I felt guilty about the daydream after that. I was afraid that maybe something bad would happen to Marilyn. I thought that in some way I had wished her dead. Even though nothing bad actually happened, I decided that daydreaming was a bad thing and that I had better stop."

Tammie was wrong. Dreaming that a thing happens doesn't mean that it actually does or will come to pass.

Tammie's daydream was a perfectly natural and healthy way for her to express the anger she had been storing up. Maybe for a minute she really did feel like pushing her friend off a cliff. But she didn't do it. She only *fantasized* about doing it. Her private thoughts could not lead to any disaster in the real world. As a matter of fact, it's a lot less dangerous to daydream about pushing someone off a cliff than it is to attempt to really do so.

Many of us often find ourselves wishing someone were dead. But this is just a fantasy and, like most fantasies, it is an undirected, fleeting image. It lasts for only a few minutes or seconds, and it is quickly forgotten. Although we all have violent fantasies, few of us have the courage to disclose them or put them into words. One reason might be that violent, angry fantasies make us feel guilty or ashamed. Or we might have been told that daydreaming is an "idle waste of time" that leads to "all sorts of trouble."

But the truth is that violent daydreams help us to release a lot of our angry, aggressive feelings. There is nothing "wrong" with letting go of angry feelings in this way. As a matter of fact, once you understand them, these fantasies can help you feel a lot better and can help you gain new awarenesses. Not all daydreams are violent, however. Here are two daydreams that helped the dreamers release some anger that they couldn't let go of in any other way.

FANTASY TO THE RESCUE

Janine is thirteen. When things get too much for her, she has the same daydream over and over again.

"My parents make rules, and in our family you obey those rules whether you like them or not, or whether they are fair or not. There's no sense arguing, because it's just not allowed. I know I'll have more privileges next year, so when my father says that I can't do this or that, I have a method that works for me. I go into the next room where I can be alone. I press my face against the window and close my eyes. Then I drift off into this fantasy world where I am the queen. *I* am the one who gives the orders. *I* make my father stay home and do my homework, and I have my older sister clean my room. I stay out late at night and order my mother to have a hot meal waiting for me and my friends. I love this fantasy. It helps me get over the anger. Afterward I feel like someone special, someone who isn't always bossed around all the time."

Josh has a favorite fantasy that he uses to help him get through the household chores he hates to do.

"I know I must be the only fourteen-year-old boy in my neighborhood who has to help his mother dust and vacuum on Saturdays. When everyone else is out playing ball, here I am at home dusting furniture like a real dope. You see, I'm an only child, and my father works six days a week. My mother was in the hospital for a long time, and we can't afford to have anyone come in and clean. So I sort of have to have to help out. But I still hate it. It makes me feel so angry to be dusting and vacuuming instead of hanging out on the corner or playing ball.

"I can't complain to my mom, because she feels bad enough. Anyway, there's nothing she can do about it. But I have one way to make things better. I fantasize that I'm this English detective, sort of a Sherlock Holmes. The house is the scene of a murder, and I am really dusting for fingerprints and searching for clues. First, I imagine what sort of murder took place and who were the suspects. I usually make it a real complicated story. Then I imagine that the murderer touched all the places where I have to dust. Once I got so involved in a 'case' that I vacuumed the living room twice without realizing it!"

Both Janine and Josh developed these fantasies as a way to help themselves get through situations that made them angry, but that they were also unable to change. Not only is nothing "bad" or "dangerous" about occasionally using a daydream to help you escape or enrich certain situations, it's a healthy coping device. Of course, many unpleasant circumstances can be changed by positive action, and too much daydreaming can be a way to avoid or to stop dealing with them. But Josh's and Janine's daydreams actually helped them cope with their angry feelings about matters over which they had no control.

THE TRUTH BEHIND THE FICTION

If we take a closer look at their fantasies, we can learn a lot more about Janine and Josh. Janine fantasized that she had power and could go places and do things. She could also order people around. That's because in her family Janine is made to feel powerless and restricted. The rules may be fair, but Janine still has the right to be angry. However, she also accepts the fact that she can't change her parents' minds about this particular issue. Instead of pushing her anger away, turning it against herself, or having a destructive temper outburst, Janine has retreated to a place where she can be angry and where she can get her way. This fantasy is important because it tells us what Janine values (freedom and power). It also helps Janine bide her time until she is older and will have more privileges.

Josh is in a different situation. He has a responsibility that he doesn't want, but he knows that expressing his anger won't help. He realizes that his mother isn't being unfair. She has no choice. But, like Janine, Josh isn't pushing his anger away. Instead, he has created a fantasy that helps make housecleaning less painful and less anger-producing for him. In Josh's fantasy, he is doing something important, something exciting, and something that demands skill and intelligence. It's obvious that Josh and Janine know what they want, but they are not yet in a position to get those things. Until they are, they can fantasize about what their lives might eventually be like by daydreaming.

For Janine and Josh, daydreaming is also a kind of temporary escape, another important function of fantasy. Sometimes you can't always have what you want when you want it. If you are a teenager, you are probably used to being told that you have to wait until you are older or an adult for certain privileges. This might make you very angry. But a little bit of fantasy can enrich your life now, and it can help make the waiting period seem shorter and less painful.

POINTING THE WAY

Some daydreams serve a very practical function—they actually help us solve problems. Fantasizing about possible solutions to difficult situations is one way to try out different methods of doing something and to decide which ones work and are really possible. Many great inventors, writers, and even scientists first thought of, and partially solved, thorny problems by fantasizing about them. This type of problem-solving daydream is a stepping stone to reality. It can give you a creative way to deal with a problem—a way you may not have thought of before. And once you are released from the restrictions of "logical" and "rational" thinking, new and different solutions may occur to you. Many of these solutions can be adapted in a very practical way to your own life.

Here is one example of a problem-solving daydream, as expressed by Luke:

"I share a bedroom with my younger brother, Gus. It's a total disaster. He leaves his things all over the floor. His clothing always manages to spread into my closet. The worst thing is that I never seem to have any privacy. Whenever I want to be with my friends, he's always there. We fight a lot. Just walking into that pigsty gets me furious. One Saturday we had a big fight about his leaving his record albums open and on my dresser. My father had to break it up. He made me sit by myself in the kitchen to 'cool off.'

"I was really angry. I wanted to break something. But, instead, I started to daydream. I imagined how nice it would be to have my room, how I'd set it up and everything. Then I just started to imagine myself fixing up the garage. I visualized myself putting up insulation and Sheetrock walls with my dad. Before I knew it, I had a solution to all my problems. I realized that my parents usually just left the car in the driveway, and with a little persuasion I'd probably be able to convince them to convert the garage. Just to make sure, I called the lumber yard and the hardware store. Then I wrote up a real professional estimate. My dad was impressed. He admitted that it was an imaginative solution that was practical, too. We agreed that my brother would probably be so glad to get rid of me that he'd pitch in and help. Now, thanks to my fantasy, I'll soon have my own room!"

TAPPING YOUR FANTASY WORLD

Daydreams, fantasies, and even nighttime dreams are all very important. They can help us to release emotions, to make unpleasant tasks bearable, and even to solve problems. Sometimes our fantasies aren't easily understood, and nighttime dreams are even more mysterious. The issues in our dreams are frequently disguised with symbols and hidden meanings. It is important to acknowledge that dreams and fantasies aren't "just a waste of time." They can serve as a springboard for understanding and working out your angry feelings, and for helping you to gain new insights about yourself.

Sometimes you may use daydreams as a way to avoid dealing with certain problems that must be faced. People who do this are apt to spend almost as much time in their dream worlds as they do in the real world. How can you tell the difference between problem-solving daydreams, emotional-release daydreams, temporary-escape daydreams, and avoidance daydreams? One way is to learn more about your own fantasies.

Keeping a journal or log of your daydreams and even your nighttime dreams can help you to understand this part of your inner life. When you are in a situation that makes you very angry, you probably have a particular type of fantasy. If you keep track of your most persistent or dramatic daydreams, you might discover that there is some message they are trying to convey to you. When you write down your daydreams, you acknowledge them in a way that can lead to greater understanding. It's also a good idea to describe the situations that might have precipitated each fantasy. After you have recorded several daydreams, look them over and ask yourself the following questions:

- How do I feel in this daydream?
- What am I trying to accomplish in this fantasy?
- Is my daydream helping me to solve a problem, release an emotion, or escape for a while?
- Was this fantasy helpful to my problem, or was it just a way to put off dealing with it?
- In my fantasy, do I make myself extra strong, extra smart, or extra good-looking?
- If so, what does this fantasy tell me about my real feelings about myself?
- Is there any way I can, or I might want to, make this fantasy come true?
- If this fantasy gave me a feeling of satisfaction, how might I be able to get this same feeling in real life?
- Might sharing this fantasy with someone else help me

feel better, learn something about myself, or accomplish my goal?

Keeping a record of your daydreams and fantasies can help you fit together some of the pieces of your inner life. Once you understand that there is nothing to fear from your dreams, you can begin to approach them as you would any other aspect of your personality. A dream log can help you to recognize recurrent themes in your dreams. After a while you will begin to see that submerged feelings of anger (and other emotions too) often find release in daydreams and nighttime dreams. It's important to have a fantasy outlet for angry and even destructive feelings.

It's all right to work out these feelings in your dream world, where you don't actually hurt anyone, and where you can feel safe and in control. If you feel that you are spending too much time in your dream world, then it's time that you took some of that energy and put it into reality problem solving. It's not healthy if your angry feelings force you into a dream world most of the time. But, for nearly all of us, it's important to set aside a specific time for drifting off and releasing hostile and aggressive feelings.

One good method is to choose a special place and time for getting in touch with these feelings. Let your mind become a mental screen for your fears, angers, and fantasies. As short a time as twenty minutes a day can refresh and replenish you because you are releasing hostile feelings that might otherwise pile up inside. This short journey to a magical place where you are in control might make you feel less angry about many of your problems.

All of us need a private place where we can be anyone we want to be and where we can say anything we want to. Many times your fantasies can be useful in your real world. They can help you to understand why you react to certain situations the way you do.

Chapter Seven

LOVE MEANS SOMETIMES HAVING TO SAY "I'M ANGRY"

People who never get angry with each other aren't being honest about their feelings. Loving or liking someone also means being able to say "Listen to me, I'm angry." But will they hear you? That doesn't depend upon how loud you shout. It depends upon what you say and how you say it.

THOSE MOVIE MYTHS

Many of us fear that if we get angry at a friend, parent, relative, or teacher, our relationship is in jeopardy. The romantic ideal pictures two lovers strolling hand in hand, starry-eyed and carefree. This has led us to believe that being in love means always being happy and always loving the other person. That's fine for the movies, but in real life things just don't work that way.

Anger is part of love. It's impossible to avoid getting angry at people you are close to. It may be that you disagree with some of their ideas. They might hurt your feelings, or they might persist with a habit that you find annoying. Holding in your anger isn't a solution. It will come out sooner or later, and that can really be confusing and destructive. When dealing with anger, the old expression "Honesty is the best policy" usually is good advice. A fight can be an expression of honest feelings between friends. It can also help to bring them closer, instead of driving them apart.

Getting angry at someone you care about can improve your relationship with that person. It can help you to keep caring about him or her, and it can help your friend to understand you more fully. But how can you express anger if you are afraid that "fighting" is a signal of a weak relationship?

The first thing you can do is to acknowledge that fighting is healthy when it is done in a *constructive manner*. No two people in the world will agree on everything. Eventually, these disagreements come to a head. That doesn't mean that you run away, or that you break up a relationship. You *can* work it out. Fighting constructively is one way to work it out, and sometimes it's the best way. True, it may not always be pleasant. You might shed a few tears in the process. But if you do it right, you can build a deeper, more lasting relationship. Since anger and fighting, even with someone you love, are inevitable, you might as well learn how to do it constructively.

It's rare in television or in the movies that we see two people who care about each other having a constructive fight. But we do see plenty of fireworks—those dramatic scenes complete with plate throwing and door slamming. All this makes for lively entertainment, but it doesn't make for a very satisfying and long-lasting relationship. Most people believe that fighting means tearing things down. Lovers have broken up and friends have parted because they have let fights turn into feuds. A feud is a fight that has been "put on ice." It is a disagreement that is not resolved and, as a result, becomes destructive to a relationship rather than constructive.

But a fight is only *temporary*. It happens when friends, people in love, or family members lock horns on a particular issue. It is *not* a signal that the relationship is a failure. It means you have a problem that will take some working out. And working it out doesn't mean simply "kissing and making up." It doesn't mean forgetting the problem and pushing it back into your memory file. Constructive fighting means confronting another person honestly and directly with your feelings. You may find yourself raising your voice. You may feel like striking out or running away. That's all part of conflict. But constructive fighting helps build relationships instead of tearing them down. You may wonder how that can be. How can fighting improve your relationships, and how can it build better understandings?

WINNING THE BATTLE, AVOIDING THE WAR

Like many other things in life, there are good and bad ways to fight. Most fights start out as harmless disagreements. Then something goes wrong and that little disagreement turns into a major battle. When this happens, you find yourself locked into a situation. Name calling, putdowns, and personal attacks can turn anger into hate. They can turn a friend into an enemy and an acquaintance into a stranger. But all fights do not have to turn out this way. What turns a fight into a war? The rules of the game, or, to be more exact, the *lack of rules*. That's right. There really are rules for arguing. Following these rules can help you avoid senseless rounds of name calling that go nowhere and have no purpose. Unfortunately, many good friendships and romances have been destroyed because the two parties involved didn't know about these rules and were unable to see that they were headed for trouble.

Learning how to fight constructively involves understanding a few simple guidelines. There aren't a lot of complicated things to memorize or study. These rules *make sense*. You won't have any trouble remembering them. But, occasionally, you might find yourself slipping back into bad patterns. That's when you'll need to remind yourself of these three simple rules:

- *State Your Needs*
- *Don't Attack the Other Person*
- *Don't Bring Up Old Wounds*

SETTING THE STAGE

"Stating your needs" means saying honestly, and without any "tricks" or manipulations, what you *want*, what you *need*, and, eventually, what you'll *settle* for. This sounds easy, but it takes a little practice. It's the first rule for fighting constructively, and it depends totally upon *you!* In most fights, no one honestly states what they really need. This causes confusion and anger. In the end, both people are arguing furiously and neither one has honestly and clearly stated exactly what they need.

What's so difficult about stating your needs? Well, for one thing, it involves a certain risk. Suppose, for example, you need to know that a certain boy or girl likes you a lot. You could try to trick them into telling you, but that usually backfires. You could state your need and tell them honestly what you feel. But you may not get the response you want. You might get rejected. This probably won't make you feel very good, but it's better than a series of elaborate tricks and games. Knowing someone else's true feelings is worthwhile in the long run, since it can prevent you from being misled and feeling foolish later on.

Another problem with stating your needs is that you may not be sure what they really are. Sometimes you may be angry at someone and begin an argument before you have taken the time to figure out your goal. Your goal should be what you *need* and *want* from that person. If you don't know those things, you can't realistically expect anyone else to.

Stating your needs means saying things like "I feel . . ." "I want . . ." and "I need . . ." and then following up those words with honest expressions that another person can respond to.

Here's a good example of two people who really care about each other. They are having a fight, but neither one is really stating his or her needs. Maybe this fight sounds like something that has happened to you:

Dina: You know, Mark, I've been thinking. Maybe we're too young to be going together.

Mark: No, we're not. All the kids are doing it.

Dina: I don't know. Maybe you'll get tired of me if we see each other so much.

Mark: Don't be silly.

Dina: It might be more fun if we sort of played the field.

Mark: You mean that you want to see other guys?

Dina: Well, only once in a while.

Mark: Look, Dina, you're my girl friend. You only go out with me. That's the way it is.

Dina: Just who do you think you are? You don't own me! If I want to see other guys, that's my business—not yours.

Mark: If that's what you want, then I'll date other girls. As a matter of fact, I know just who I'll ask to that party Friday night.

Dina: Who—Jennifer?

Mark: That's my business. Remember you don't own me either. You started this, so now you know how it feels!

Dina: You really know how to be obnoxious!

Mark: I must have learned it from you!

Dina: I wouldn't be your girl friend if you were the last boy left in the world!

Mark: Forget I ever asked you!

Dina: I'll forget you, too!
Mark: That's just fine with me!

If Mark and Dina sound familiar, it's probably because you, too, have been involved in this sort of destructive fight. It doesn't matter "who started it" or whose "fault" the fight was. In the end, both parties suffer.

What went wrong in this particular fight? If you take a second look, you'll see that neither Mark nor Dina ever stated their needs or feelings. No one bothered to say, "I need . . ." "I want . . ." "I feel . . ." Dina never told Mark how she really felt about going with him. She only hinted that it would be more "fun" if they dated other people. That didn't leave Mark much to respond to. He assumed he was being rejected, so he responded with anger.

At this point, Mark could have shared his feelings with Dina. He could have told her how her words made him feel. But, instead, he began to order her around and tell her what she could and could not do. At this point the angry games and manipulations began. Dina and Mark both tried to trick each other into expressing feelings of jealousy, affection, and, eventually, hate. At no time did they pause and attempt to state their real needs. Did Dina really want to break up with Mark, or was she just trying to make him jealous? If so, why did she want to do this in the first place? Was Mark really a bossy, possessive guy who secretly wanted to go out with another girl?

We have no way of knowing. And the sad thing is that neither do they. Finally, the relationship was damaged, and maybe even destroyed, because Mark and Dina didn't know the rules of constructive fighting. They fought destructively and did *not* state their needs. Let's take a look at how things might have been.

Dina: You know, Mark, I've been thinking. Maybe we're too young to be going together.

Mark: No, we're not. All the kids are doing it.

Dina: I don't know. Maybe you'll get tired of me if we see each other so much.

Mark: Don't be silly.

Dina: It might be more fun if we sort of played the field.

Mark: Are you saying that you want to see other guys?

Dina: Well, only once in a while.

Mark: Dina, I really like you a lot. But this is making me angry. I also feel hurt. I'm not sure, but I think you're saying that you don't want to be my girl friend.

Dina: No, that's not what I'm saying at all. I'm sorry that I hurt you, because I like you a lot too. I just feel a little scared of the commitment involved in seeing only one boy.

Mark: What do you mean "scared"?

Dina: Well, I feel that if we spend so much time together, you'll get tired of me.

Mark: You know, I feel the same way. I feel a little afraid too.

Dina: Do you think that this means we don't really care enough about each other?

Mark: I don't know for sure, but I don't think so.

Dina: I don't think so either, but what should we do?

Mark: Dina, I like you more than any other girl. I know I love being with you, and it would hurt me if you dated other boys. So why don't we give going steady a try. After all, it's not like getting married or anything.

Dina: I guess you're right. I think I needed to hear you tell me how much you really cared. Let's try it and see what happens.

The difference is obvious. Mark and Dina began the argument the same way, but something turned this fight around. Something happened that brought the two people closer instead of driving them apart. In this case Mark and Dina took a few risks. Instead of playing silly and cruel games with each other, they talked about their true *feelings* and *needs*. Mark told Dina what he felt. She responded with her own feelings. Both parties stated what they needed—reassurance that the other one cared enough to take the risk of making a commitment.

But it takes two people to turn a destructive fight into a constructive one. That means being able to listen and being willing to respond with words like "I need . . ." and "I feel . . ." instead of attacking with words like "You are . . ." "You do . . ." or "Everyone says that you . . ." Attacking the other person will only result in a return of hostility. And this brings us to the second rule of constructive fighting.

DON'T GET SIDETRACKED

One of the most obvious mistakes we can make when we're angry is to attack someone else. We begin by arguing about a specific incident and wind up making nasty comments about the other person's personality, way of life, even family and friends.

This kind of provocation is hard for anyone to resist.

Name calling almost always results in a painful situation and a destructive fight. No one likes to be made fun of, and very few people have the self-control to turn the other cheek and walk away. So it makes sense to *stick to the issues*. This means arguing about a specific problem and not allowing yourself to get sidetracked. Attacking the way another person looks, talks, or behaves is one sure way to turn a disagreement into a war.

How can you avoid this destructive tendency? By becoming aware of the problem and by exerting some self-control. When you are having a fight, it's up to you to catch yourself when you automatically slip into this pattern. One signal that you could be slipping is the use of expressions like "You are . . ." "Everybody says that you . . ." and "Just because you . . ." What usually follows is a series of cutting remarks about the other person. It's important to remember that when you attack the other person, *even if what you are saying about them is true*, you make it impossible to reach your goals and to resolve the fight in a constructive manner. Here's an example of a fight between a father and son in which personal attacks overshadow the real issues:

Father: Well, David, it's getting close to graduation. I wish you'd make up your mind and choose a college.

David: Dad, I already told you, I'm not going to college. I want to look for a job as a photographer's assistant.

Father: Yes, you've told me that, and a lot of other things, but I don't agree with any of them. Now, the time has come for a real decision.

David: It's decided. I'm not going to college.

Father: Be realistic. If you go to college, you can go into business and earn a good living and be secure for the rest of your life.

David: Look, Dad, that's the way you did it, but that doesn't mean I have to do it the same way.

Father: That's right, and I did a pretty good job of it. You never complained about not having anything you wanted.

David: True, but look how boring your life is. All you ever do is work, work, work. Everyone knows that. You never do anything exciting, just drag into the same old job day after day. You don't even have any outside interests.

Father: Just what do you mean by that? I have no time for hobbies.

David: Exactly, you're becoming a boring person. All you ever think about is money and financial security. Nobody finds that interesting. I don't want to wind up like you.

Father: Well, how ungrateful can you get! I noticed you never complained about me being boring when you wanted a new car, or that fancy stereo. We'll see how exciting you'll be when you're unemployed and come to your boring father for a handout.

David: So, it's either your way or nothing? Well, I'd rather starve than wind up working in a dull, routine job like yours.

Father: Since you feel that way, I'll help you get used to poverty right now. You can forget about your allowance and about getting any help from me from now on!

David wanted to get an important point across to his

father. He wanted to tell him about his plans for the future. David's father might have listened. But it was pretty difficult for him to hear anything other than the personal attack that David launched. By calling his father "boring" and making fun of his job and way of life, David was attacking the other person. He wasn't arguing about the real issues. This tactic worked against him. It prevented him from reaching his goal, which was to convince his father that what he wanted to do after graduation was acceptable. And it also damaged his relationship with his father.

David's father responded to this attack by punishing him. Neither David nor his father listened to one another or tried to get the argument back to the real issues involved. In the end, they both lost and were driven even further apart. It would have been a lot easier if both parties had known the rules of constructive fighting. Let's see how this fight might have been if those rules had been followed:

Father: Well, David, it's getting close to graduation. I wish you'd make up your mind and choose a college.

David: Dad, I've told you. I'm not going to college. I want to look for a job as a photographer's assistant.

Father: Yes, you've told me that, and a lot of other things, but I don't agree with any of them. Now, the time has come for a real decision.

David: I don't want to go to college.

Father: Be realistic. If you go to college, you can go into business, earn a good living, and be secure for the rest of your life.

David: That may be true. That's how things worked for

you. But I'm different. At this stage of my life, I have to figure out what's best for *me*. I feel I have to make my own decisions and my own mistakes.

Father: But, David, you know that if you go to college, it will just be a matter of time before you get a good job. Things are tough enough. How much money can a photographer expect to make? A good job will give you financial security.

David: I understand what you're saying, but there are other things that I feel I need to have.

Father: Like what?

David: Like doing something I find interesting, diversified, and fulfilling.

Father: Do you really think that a job, even as a photographer, can be all that?

David: Well, I don't know. But I think I owe it to myself to try and find out.

Father: But you may miss out on college in that search.

David: I'm only seventeen. I have lots of time ahead of me. I can explore and still go back to school and have financial security and a family later on.

Father: Well, consider yourself lucky. In my day, we didn't have the luxury to explore and experiment.

David: Times have changed. Lucky for me. But, Dad, it's important to me that you see my way of thinking and give me a chance and a little encouragement. That's what I really need.

Father: Well, it's certainly not the way I would do things, but I guess you'll have to live your life the way you want to. You may regret this decision, but I'll just have to stand by you for a while.

David: Thanks, Dad.

Unlike the first argument, this one was resolved constructively. It helped both David and his father work together. What went right this time? Neither David nor his father attacked each other personally, despite the fact that they were feeling anger. There was no name calling. No one used expressions like "You are . . ." or "Everybody says that you are . . ." In this argument David stayed with the main issue. As a result, his father was able to react to his son's logic rather than to his anger. Although David's father still doesn't agree with his son's choice of a career, hearing David's defense of it makes him willing to go along with it for a while longer. That's a lot better for David, and a lot better for the relationship.

LET BYGONES BE BYGONES

Old wounds leave scars. But a scar is a sign of healing. If you open up an old wound, it will take even longer until the healing process can begin again. Emotional wounds work the same way. When something upsetting happens to you, it can take a long time until the memory (the wound) begins to fade. You never really forget a painful emotional experience. A small trace, like a scar, always remains. We all need time to heal from both physical and emotional wounds. This means that sometimes you have to deal with the present instead of going back into the past and opening up old wounds.

When you're angry, you might ignore this healing process. You might try to recall and bring up every bad thing that ever happened to you. You can use these memories to make a fight a destructive and painful experience. Bringing up old wounds means using expressions like "You always . . ." "You never . . ." "Every time . . ." and "I remember the time when you . . ." These expressions cloud the present issue. They confuse what is happening *right now* with what might have happened two days or even two years ago. *Arguing about the present issue* is another important rule of constructive fighting. Here's a common example of two people who break that rule and turn an argument into a destructive fight:

Mother: Ellen, please take out the garbage.
Ellen: Not right now, Mom. I'm busy.
Mother: Ellen, I wish you'd drop what you're doing for five minutes and take care of this garbage!
Ellen: I'll do it when I'm finished with this.
Mother: No, you won't. You'll forget, so do it now!
Ellen: Please, leave me alone. Why am I always the one you ask? Why don't you make Karen or Stuart do this?
Mother: Why do you always have to fight with me? You never listen to anything I say. Take out this garbage, and no more back talk!
Ellen: There you go again! Picking on me as usual. I'm always being picked on in this house. Don't think I forgot about that time you made me clean up Stuart's mess.
Mother: You never do as you're told. You've been like this since you were a baby.
Ellen: That's not true! I remember all the times that you were unfair. You always favor Karen and Stuart. I remember that horrible time when you . . .

This is one fight that really goes nowhere. It will probably result in a screaming match between Ellen and her mother. And no matter who takes out the garbage, both people will be pretty miserable. It's not always easy to avoid saying things like "I remember the time when . . ." or "You always . . ." But you will be in a stronger position if you simply stick to the present and try not to build up a case against someone based on what they might or might not have done in the past. If you do go back to the past, you'll probably wind up like Ellen and her mother— arguing about something that happened a long time ago instead of discussing a solution for the present.

Staying with the present means that you'll be able to *hear* what the other person *needs* and *wants* and you'll be able to *respond* with what you need and want. Both of you will be *listening* instead of *defending* yourselves against crimes of the past. When you feel someone else opening up an old wound, it's a lot easier to say, "Let's talk about *right now*," than it is to get carried away in a pointless and destructive fight. Here's how Ellen and her mother could have avoided that situation:

Mother: Ellen, please take out the garbage.

Ellen: Not right now, Mom. I'm busy.

Mother: Ellen, I wish you'd drop what you're doing for a minute and take out this garbage.

Ellen: I'll do it as soon as I'm finished with this.

Mother: You'll probably forget, so please do it now.

Ellen: I won't forget. I wish that you'd trust me to do it.

Mother: It has nothing to do with trust. I want something done and I don't see why I have to have an argument about it.

Ellen: I feel that you aren't being fair to me. Can't you ask Karen to do it?

Mother: Karen washes the dinner dishes.

Ellen: OK. But what would be so bad if I took the garbage out in an hour—at six o'clock. After all, they don't pick it up until tomorrow morning.

Mother: Nothing would be bad about that except that if you don't do it now, you never will.

Ellen: Well, I promise I will take it out at six. I want you to trust me. Why don't you give me a chance?

Mother: Believe me, I have given you lots of chances.

Ellen: That may be true, but let's talk about *now*.

Mother: OK. But that garbage better be taken out at six o'clock sharp!

Ellen and her mother broke the pattern of bringing up old angers and opening old wounds. They both stayed with the present and avoided words like "You always . . ." "You never . . ." and "I remember the time when . . ." It helped them to defuse a potentially destructive fight. In this fight both people *heard* and *listened*. They were each satisfied with the result. Of course, not all arguments can be resolved exactly like this one. But you can avoid going back into the past and getting so far off the track that any resolution of differences becomes impossible.

PUTTING THEORY TO PRACTICE

Stating your needs, not opening up old wounds, and not attacking the other person are easy to talk about, but not always so easy to do in real life. That's because, for most of us, destructive ways of fighting have become ingrained patterns of behavior. We do them almost automatically. In a way, that makes us prisoners. It makes us unable to change our own behavior and to improve our relationships with other people.

Changing your patterns takes time. But it is the only way you can be free to express your feelings and to listen to other people express theirs. When you're no longer a prisoner of your own patterns, you can truly hear what your father, mother, or friends have to say. And once you begin to listen to them, there's a good chance they'll be able to hear you, too!

Chapter Eight

THE OTHER SIDE OF DISHING IT OUT . . . TAKING IT

I can take it...

In the case of anger it's definitely easier to give than it is to receive. But as the saying goes, "If you can dish it out, you'd better learn how to take it!" Although anger involves a lot more than simply "giving" and "taking," when someone is angry with you it can seem as if your whole world is falling apart. Their anger may cause you to feel guilt, fear, rage, humiliation, or any combination of these emotions. It's no surprise that most of us would do just about anything to avoid having our friends, teachers, parents, or brothers and sisters get angry with us.

DON'T BE DEFENSIVE

When anger is being directed toward you, it almost always feels as if you are being attacked. When this happens, your first impulse is usually to defend yourself. However, acting defensively is probably the worst way you can respond to someone else's anger. A defensive response is a destructive way of protecting yourself. It means that you won't allow the angry feelings to touch you. But if you can't be touched, you can't hear the other person's needs and you'll be unable to respond to them in an effective manner. When you run to your own defense, you avoid taking responsibility for your actions.

Denying that you did something to cause an angry response means denying someone else's right to say "Listen to me, I'm angry." Because a defensive response is so automatic, it's important to know when you are acting this way. Expressions like "It wasn't me . . ." "I didn't do it . . ." "I was forced to do it . . ." "I had no choice . . ." "If it wasn't for . . ." and "It's all his (or her) fault . . ." are clear indications that you are hiding behind your own defenses. Although becoming defensive may seem like the "natural" thing to do, it isn't always the best way to deal with someone else's anger.

SIT BACK AND LISTEN

Listening is the most constructive tool you have. It's not something that is done passively or accidentally. It's a skill that takes practice and effort. But, even more important, listening is the best way to respond when someone is expressing anger toward you.

Most of us feel uncomfortable and even guilty when we are told that something we've done is "wrong," "bad," or "hurtful." The first impulse may be to answer back, to deny it, or to defend yourself. But listening is the only way you can really understand what the other person is saying. To be an effective listener takes discipline. It means putting aside your first impulsive reaction and "hearing someone else out."

They may say things that make you angry and you may just be "itching" to show them how unfair and how wrong they really are. But when you do this, you set up a destructive pattern. You answer back. They retaliate. And before you know it, you're embroiled in a war of angry, hurtful feelings. In order to avoid this, you'll have to use self-control and listen. When the other person has finished (and, hopefully, cooled down), it's your turn to take the next step.

SIFTING AND SORTING

Clarifying means making things easier to understand. To do this, you must separate *facts* from *feelings*. When things are unclear, they are mixed-up, cloudy, and con-fusing. In an argument, feelings of anger, guilt, and pain usually confuse the real issues and make them more difficult to understand. That's why it's important to clarify those issues, especially when someone is angry with you. How do you clarify when you are the target of someone's anger?

One way is by trying to work things out aloud. Ask the other person to repeat or to explain some of the things he or she is saying. This can be done diplomatically by stating, "I hear you saying that you're very angry with me," or, "I think that you believe what I did was unfair." In most cases you'll have to do this more than once before you have clearly separated, in your own mind, the facts from the feelings. It's important to let the other person know what you are trying to do and why. When you have clarified things, you'll have a pretty good idea of why the other person is furious. Now you should communicate that understanding. Let the other person know that you have heard and understood their anger. They will take some satisfaction in knowing that you are willing to deal with their feelings.

One way of communicating is to state clearly what you think the main problem is. If, for example, your older sister is furious that you have borrowed her sweater without asking, you might say, "I understand that you're angry at me because I wore your sweater without asking."

Although this sounds easy, it's a step that most of us never take. Instead, we avoid the main issue and use tactics to distract and trick the other person. Instead of letting your sister know that you understand why she is angry with you, you might, for example, bring up a time when she borrowed something of yours without asking. You might deny that you borrowed the sweater, or you might tell her to stop making such a "big thing" out of it. If you've tried these tactics, then you know what happens next. The other person, in this case your older sister, blows up and an all-out battle ensues. It's important to clarify and to communicate. But that's not enough. Next, you'll need to sort out the other person's needs.

DISCOVERING YOUR ROLE

Once you have listened and understood why someone is angry with you, you have to figure out what it is he or she wants. Why are they bringing these feelings to you? What do they need? There is always a reason, a demand, or a need behind every confrontation. Sometimes, if you're lucky, the person you're fighting with will be honest and state these needs. But this is the exception rather than the rule. Most of the time they only show you their fury.

It's up to you to get them to tell you what you can do about it. Sometimes it's just a simple apology. Other times they just want you to listen. But, in many cases, someone may be asking or demanding that you change your behavior in some way. You may have to give up something, make a compromise, or promise never to do a particular thing again. That's where the tough part comes in. That's where you have to decide what's being asked of you and how, or if, you can respond to that request.

THREE DIFFERENT ENDINGS

Should you meet the other person's demands? The answer is yes when you feel that the demands are reasonable. If you are confronted with the fact that your behavior has caused someone to feel angry or hurt, it's reasonable for you to assume responsibility for your behavior. Simply saying "Yes, I did borrow your sweater without asking," or "No, I didn't call you when I knew I was going to be late" is the best way to acknowledge that you are taking responsibility for your own behavior. (Unless, of course, you really didn't do it.)

In many cases it may also be reasonable to meet the other person's demands. Sometimes all a person wants is an apology. At other times people may want you to explain why you did a particular thing. Certain friends may just need you to listen to their angry feelings and let them know that you'll still care even if they do get angry once in a while. But most of the time another person will want you to change your behavior in some way. Saying yes to any of these things is up to you. Is the request *reasonable*? Is it something you won't feel guilty or angry about doing? Will doing it help maintain or improve your relationship with that person? These are just some of the questions you should ask yourself before you decide to meet someone else's demands.

Maybe you need a little time. Sometimes even a simple apology can be difficult. It might seem that you are "giving in" and "swallowing your pride." In that case, reassure your friend or relative that you understand the problem, but that you need time to be alone with your own feelings before you can decide what to do. Saying yes can be complicated and confusing. It sometimes means acknowledging that you were wrong or thoughtless. It might mean giving up something or changing your behavior in some way. When, and if, you do decide to say yes to another person's demands, it should mean that you have taken a good look at the situation and at your own feelings and needs.

Someone once said that the word "no" is the most difficult word in the English language. That person was probably right. When someone is angry with you, it's all too easy to give in to their demands. You know if you say yes the fight will be over and forgotten. But saying no means that the other person may get even angrier. It's no fun when you decide to say no, but it's your right and it's an important right.

Too often we forfeit our right to say no because we're afraid. This fear is a result of thinking that saying no to a person's demand is the same thing as rejecting that person. Of course, no one likes to be rejected or to reject a relative or friend. But sometimes saying no is a necessity. It doesn't mean you are rejecting another person. It only means that what they are asking of you is more than you are willing or able to give. There is only one way to learn how to say no and that's through practice. But once acquired, this important skill will actually help you to build better relationships with other people.

Saying yes or saying no isn't the only way to resolve a disagreement. There may also be a compromise solution. Working out a compromise means giving up part of what you want in exchange for an agreement you can live with. When it's possible (and it isn't always), a compromise plan is probably the best way to work out a problem. That's because each person gets part of what they want and need. No one "wins" or "loses" an argument that is resolved with a satisfactory compromise agreement.

But there is an art to compromise. It involves negotiating

—listening and discussing your problem with the other person. If you're burning with anger, you won't have the presence of mind needed to really listen to the other person's needs. That's why a compromise may take a few hours or even weeks to work out. Both parties must be willing and able to listen to each other. They both have to think about what they are giving up and what they will gain in the long run. When done thoughtfully, a compromise plan helps resolve the argument, calm the anger, and build a deeper understanding between friends.

TURNING TO REAL LIFE

Now that you know the ground rules of constructive fighting and have some idea of how to deal with someone else's anger, you're ready to see how these ideas work in an actual fight. Here's an example of two friends who are having a heated argument. In this case, Jan is on the receiving end of her friend Sandy's anger. But instead of acting defensively, Jan has decided to deal with her friend's anger by listening, clarifying, communicating, and sorting out needs. Let's see what happens.

On Wednesday, Jan and Sandy made plans to go to the movies together the following Saturday. Saturday morning Jan arrived at Sandy's house. Here's what followed:

Sandy: Hi, Jan. You're early. I'm almost ready—give me a few more minutes.

Jan: Sandy, I have something to tell you. I won't be able to go to the movies with you today.

Sandy: Why not?

Jan: Well, last night Paul called me. You know how much I like him. He wanted to know if I'd go with him to the school football game this afternoon. I said yes. That's why I can't go to the movies with you.

Sandy: Wow! I can't believe it. I can't believe that you would do that to me. Some friend you turned out to be. You're just boy crazy. We were planning to go to the movies since early this week. I can see it very clearly. You don't care about me at all. I'm just someone to be with when you don't have a date. I'm glad I found out what kind of a friend you really are. I'm really a poor judge of character. How can you possibly stand there and tell me this?

Jan: I understand that you're furious at me.

Sandy: That's an understatement!

Jan: I hear you saying that you're furious and you feel that what I've done is unfair and inconsiderate.

Sandy: Unfair, inconsiderate, hostile, bitchy—the list goes on forever!

Jan: You feel that I didn't think of you and that I only thought of myself.

Sandy: You said it!

Jan: I guess you don't think I was a very good friend.

Sandy: I think you were a terrible, disloyal friend.

Jan: I understand your anger and I would feel the same way if you had done it to me.

Sandy: I don't understand. Why in the world did you do it if you knew how I'd feel?

Jan: Because I really like Paul a lot, too. I've been hoping he'd ask me out for months. But you know that he's never seemed to notice me. Then yesterday, out of the clear blue sky, he called me. I was so excited that I immediately said yes.

Sandy: Without considering our plans or my feelings!

Jan: That's right. I was so anxious to go out with Paul that I completely disregarded our plans. I was wrong, and I'm sorry. I care a lot about you and I consider you my best friend, but the truth is that at the time I was thinking more about my needs than yours. Now I feel very bad about the way I behaved.

Sandy: Well, I'm glad that you can at least admit that you were wrong. But you've broken our plans, and I feel hurt and disappointed. Now I have nothing at all to do this afternoon.

Jan: You're right, Jan, I have a commitment and a responsibility to you for today. I only broke it because I was afraid that if I said no to Paul, he wouldn't call me again. But I'll call him and explain everything. We'll go to the movies together as we had planned.

Sandy: You'd do that for me? Really?

Jan: Yes. It's really the only thing I can do.

Sandy: Jan, now that you've explained why you did it, I feel better. The fact that you'd break your date with Paul makes me feel that you're really a good friend, after all. I guess I'd have had a tough time if I had been in your situation. It's all right. I know you've waited for him to ask you out for a long time. Go ahead to the football game. I'll find something else to do.

Jan: Sandy, you really are my best friend. Thanks for understanding and putting up with me!

This is a good example of a fight that brought two people closer together. It worked out this way because

Jan understood the rules of constructive fighting. She applied them, and Sandy responded. Let's take a closer look and see exactly what happened.

When Jan told Sandy about the change in plans, Sandy immediately became enraged. She began to attack Jan by claiming that she wasn't a good friend, that she was "boy crazy," and that she "used" her to fill in when she didn't have a date. Jan responded by *listening*. It probably wasn't easy, but she did. She didn't become defensive. Jan let Sandy express her rage, and she never tried to deny that she was boy crazy or a bad friend. At this time, it would have only made Sandy angrier and gotten the fight off the real issues.

As soon as Sandy ran out of steam and seemed more able to listen, Jan tried to *clarify*. She tried to separate the facts from the feelings. She used expressions like "I hear what you're saying . . ." and "You feel that . . ." Jan then communicated the fact that she understood why Sandy was angry at her. At that point it was clear that both girls were talking about the same issue. They weren't fighting about whether or not Jan was a bad friend or boy crazy. Sandy's angry confrontation caused Jan to think about her behavior. She realized that what she had done was selfish and inconsiderate. Once that was clear, she took responsibility for her behavior. She sorted out her needs and her friend's needs. She made a *decision* to meet Sandy's demands and to cancel her date with Paul.

Remember how enraged Sandy was at the beginning of this fight? That was very different from the way she felt by the end of the argument. What happened? Sandy was allowed to express her angry feelings because Jan *listened, didn't get defensive*, and *didn't interrupt* with old wounds or personal attacks. Sandy was free to say all that she was feeling. She also felt that her anger was accepted and taken seriously. No one told her to "shut up" or not to "make a big thing out of it." Finally Sandy's needs were met. Jan apologized, shared her feelings, and agreed to cancel her date with Paul.

What saved this fight and this friendship was the fact that the two friends listened to each other and met each other's needs. Once Jan told Sandy that she was willing to break the date, Sandy realized that her friend really cared for her. That was enough for Sandy. She needed a loyal friend who cared enough to consider her feelings. Once she knew that Jan was that kind of friend, she was able to give something back to her. That was when she told Jan to go out with Paul, after all.

This friendship was saved because Jan knew how to fight constructively. She didn't run away from Sandy's angry feelings. And Sandy did not push Jan to prove herself and accept her offer to cancel her date with Paul. This shows that Sandy understood and accepted Jan's needs. In this particular fight, one person decided to say yes to another person's demands. But what happens when you fight constructively and then decide to say no? Let's take a look at that kind of fight.

WHEN THE ANSWER IS NO

Jeff and Karen have been going together for eight months. Recently Jeff broke his guitar and had to send it to the shop to be repaired. This weekend he is going camping with his friends and he would like to bring a guitar with him. Guess whose guitar he has in mind?

Jeff: Karen, would you mind if I borrowed your guitar for the weekend?

Karen: I would like to lend it to you, Jeff, but I saved up a long time for it and it's very important to me. I really don't feel right about lending it out to people.

Jeff: I'm not people. I'm your boy friend. You can trust me.

Karen: I don't think I should, Jeff. I know if I lend it to you, I'll be worried about it all weekend.

Jeff: Look, Karen, I had a guitar for five years. I know how to take care of it.

Karen: I'm sorry, Jeff. I have to say no.

Jeff: I don't believe it! I'm really hurt and angry that you don't trust me enough to lend me your guitar. It makes me wonder what kind of a girl friend you really are!

Karen: I understand why you feel hurt and angry. You feel I have let you down and that I don't trust you with my guitar.

Jeff: That's right. I'm beginning to think that you don't even care about me either!

Karen: I do care about you—a lot. I think that I'm a loyal and considerate girl friend. But sometimes I need to be a friend to myself first. I just have to say no even though you don't like to hear it.

Jeff: But why do you have to say no this weekend?

Karen: I don't think it has anything to do with this week-end. It has to do with the issue of my guitar. Would you really want me to say yes when I didn't mean it, or want to, just because I was afraid to be honest?

Jeff: Well—I guess not.

Karen: No, I didn't think so. Sometimes I have to say no. This is just one of those times.

Jeff: I still don't like it and I'm very disappointed.

Karen: I understand what you're saying. But it doesn't mean that I like you any less for it. It's just one of those times when what you want is different from what I want. We are, after all, two separate people. If there was a way I could compromise, I would. But, Jeff, there's no way you can borrow half a guitar!

Jeff: I see what you mean. I guess we just disagree on this issue. Maybe I can borrow Bruce's guitar.

This fight is an example of what can happen when someone says no. Jeff wanted to borrow the guitar from Karen. Maybe it was a simple request. But Karen didn't think so. Her guitar meant a lot to her. She knew that her weekend would be ruined because she would be worried about what might happen. So she said no. Jeff reacted the way most people would. He felt hurt and angry. Karen separated her *feelings* from the *facts*. She explained to Jeff that she cared for him and trusted him, but that in this case she had to be a friend to herself, too. Karen knows that saying no is part of who she is. She understands that she and Jeff are different people and it's only natural that they will disagree on certain issues sometimes. She tried to help Jeff understand this too.

In the end, both acknowledged that a compromise plan wouldn't work. Jeff saw that Karen was trying to communicate with him. He was able to separate his feelings from the facts and he saw another possible solution that didn't involve borrowing Karen's guitar.

OTHER REWARDS

Once you can cope with a friend's angry feelings toward you, you can be sure that you're learning how to cope with your own anger. It's easy to slide back into name calling and opening up old wounds. But these tactics never work. Acknowledging that anger is a legitimate emotion that need not be destructive is the first step toward learning how to deal with it. Some of the fights in the preceding chapters may seem familiar to you. That's because almost everyone has tried to run away from their own anger or from someone else's anger at one time or another.

Even if you follow all the rules of constructive fighting, there are bound to be times when you have a destructive fight that leads nowhere. But in most cases the ideas and guidelines you have just read about *can* help. They can make a difference between a fight and a war, and between anger and hatred. You will discover that the more you learn about feelings in general, the more you learn about yourself in particular. And once you have learned to accept your own anger, it will become easier and less frightening to deal with other people's anger.

Chapter Nine

COPING

There are times when all the talking and good intentions in the world can't change things. There are times when you're angry and you can't do a thing about it. These are the times when you feel furious at the entire world, not anyone in particular. This kind of anger is difficult to cope with. It feels as though there is nothing you can do to make it go away. It seems that it will last forever. That's because there's no one to fight, no way to shake it.

DEATH AND MOURNING

Death makes us sad. It also makes us angry. When you lose someone you love, there is a feeling of emptiness inside. You miss seeing and sharing your life with a special friend or relative. You might think, deep down, that it was unfair for that person to leave you. You might wonder how he or she could die when you needed and depended upon them so much. You might feel that you "can't go on living" or that life will be "empty and meaningless now." These are common reactions to the death of someone who has been close to you.

Feeling angry when someone you love dies is a natural reaction to a very real loss. But in most cases you are only in touch with the sad feelings. Friends and relatives recall all the good things about the person who has passed away. This is part of mourning. But sometimes this can make it more difficult for you to express the deep anger you are feeling. Death *is* unfair. And you *are* helpless to do anything about changing it. You have a right to feel angry about your loss. Your anger won't change anything, but that doesn't mean you should be ashamed to talk about it. Anger is a natural part of the process of mourning.

Feeling depressed is another unavoidable part of mourning. It, too, is a natural result of that same helpless feeling. Although no one can say how long it should last, depression does end. At first it is very intense. It may even interfere with your life. Going to school, seeing friends, and playing sports may seem impossible when you feel this way. But the feelings *do* pass slowly. After a while they will not be as strong. This doesn't mean that you have forgotten the person who died. It just means that you have passed through the period of mourning.

DIVORCE

As a teenager, you are really still your parents' child. You may feel ready to live on your own and to make your own rules, but it's doubtful that you'll get that chance. Decisions that your parents make also affect you. In many cases, these decisions are made without your input. But they can have a dramatic effect upon your life. Divorce is one of those decisions.

When parents decide to live apart, it's because life together has become unbearable. This is a painful and difficult step for them to take. They might discuss it with you, but, in the end, it is *their* decision. When parents divorce or separate, you lose something too. You may have to relocate, change schools, or move in with a relative. You may also see your mother or father a lot less than you did before. No matter what happens, things *will* be different.

Divorce is difficult for everyone in the family. You may understand your parents' decision. You may even agree with it. But that doesn't mean that you won't feel angry about the changes that occur in your life because of it. Sometimes you may feel that the rest of the world lives in happy two-parent families. Television shows that portray "all-American" family situations may make you resentful about your parents' divorce. You might feel cheated and different because your parents couldn't get along.

These feelings are understandable, but they are often difficult to express. It may be hard to tell your parents because they seem to have so many problems of their own. You might even feel a little guilty. Maybe, deep down, you worry that *you* may have caused your family to break up. Worrying about your future, your guilt, and the changes in your life can make you very angry. If you believe that you don't have a right to express that anger, you are likely to become confused and depressed.

One way to avoid this is to share your feelings with someone who knows how to listen. The important thing to remember is that divorce is painful. It does hurt. Don't try to act as if nothing has changed. When your parents split up, you'll feel many things. Anger is one of them. It's natural that you should feel angry and, what's more important, it's your right to have these feelings and to express them.

WHEN NOTHING CAN BE DONE

Death and divorce are only two of many situations that can cause feelings of helpless rage. Unwanted pregnancy, physical handicaps, accidents, and other unexpected occurrences may make you feel confused and angry. They can make you feel that life is "unfair." But in these cases there is no one to blame, no one to fight with, and no way to undo what has already happened.

In these instances, friends and relatives might try to comfort you with expressions like "Be brave," or "Grin and bear it." They might try to remind you that other people are less fortunate and that you should be thankful for what you *do* have. Although people mean well when they say these things, their comments often make you feel even worse. That's because these expressions usually have little to do with your real feelings, which are probably more like anger and fear than courage and gratitude.

If you have suffered a disabling accident, have been born with a handicap, or have experienced a sudden physical change (anything from acne to pregnancy), it's normal to be angry. Even though other people may not like to hear about them, it's important that you express those feelings.

One teenager who lost her hearing as a result of a progressive illness describes her situation this way:

"I had known for a few years that I was slowly going deaf. But aside from going to doctors, I never really dealt with the situation. When it finally happened, I wasn't emotionally prepared. I was furious that it had to happen to me. Being trapped in a silent world with nothing but my own rage was almost unbearable. I needed someone to help me cope with my feelings about being deaf just as much as I needed to cope with the deafness itself."

Another teenager, who discovered she was pregnant, found that her anger prevented her from dealing with the situation in a rational manner. Here's what she experienced:

"I couldn't believe it was true! One little mistake and now I had to suffer the consequences. I was ashamed and embarrassed, but mostly I was furious. How could I have been so careless? Why me? I felt like a victim. I was angry at the whole world. There were plenty of people who wanted to help me. But I shut them all out. I had no one to direct my anger at, so I turned it inward and began hating myself. Luckily, someone got through to me before I did something I know I would have regretted."

WHO CAN HELP?

Coping with anger often means reaching out for help. Death, divorce, physical handicaps, and accidents are some of life's painful experiences. They can cause you to feel helpless and angry. Sometimes old angers that have not been expressed build up and cause feelings of depression. As times goes by, these feelings can get worse. They might result in destructive behavior. Everyone feels depressed and angry from time to time. But if you have been experiencing these emotions more than just once in a while, you may need to reach out for some expert help.

The mental health profession doesn't only deal with "crazies" or people in hospitals. Plenty of normal men and women, girls and boys, parents and teachers, doctors and lawyers turn to this profession to help them cope with problems. The mental health profession consists of counselors, psychologists, social workers, psychiatrists, and psychoanalysts. All these people do psychotherapy of one sort or another.

WHAT IS PSYCHOTHERAPY?

Psychotherapy doesn't mean "getting your head shrunk." You won't be hypnotized or forced to recall your earliest memories. All psychotherapists do is listen, talk, and listen some more. Although there are many different types of therapy, talking and listening are the only tools of a good therapist. But you may ask yourself, "Why go to a shrink when I can talk to my friend or to my mom?"

The answer is simple. Listening is a carefully developed skill. Although your friend or your mother may care about you and want to help, they may not know how. A therapist is trained (and this training can take more than six years) to listen and ask questions that will help you discover the roots of your problems as well as their solutions.

WHAT TO EXPECT

When you visit a therapist, you can feel free to talk about anything and everything. You don't have to worry about hurting his or her feelings and you don't have to worry about getting in trouble for what you say. Anything you tell a therapist is *strictly confidential.* Nothing you say can be repeated to parents, teachers, or law enforcement agencies. Love, sex, hate, the past, the present, the future, drinking, smoking, mothers, fathers, friends, enemies, and the way you feel about therapy itself are some of the things you can discuss in your sessions.

That's because the goal of therapy is to set you free. Once you have explained and clarified your feelings, you are on the way to understanding and accepting them. When this happens, you no longer have to keep everything bottled up inside. At the end of (and even during) a successful therapy experience you will feel free—intellectually, sexually, and most of all emotionally.

No one can predict how long *your* therapy will take.

The length of treatment depends on you. If you enter therapy as a result of an immediate crisis in your life, you may only need a few sessions to work things out. Some people, however, begin therapy because they want to make changes in their personality. They might be depressed, have psychosomatic illnesses or drug or alcohol problems, or want to overcome feelings of shyness or fear. This kind of therapy takes longer since it must get to the root—the cause—of the problem.

The length of a therapy session is usually forty-five minutes to an hour. Most people attend one to three times weekly. The sessions can be informative, satisfying, and helpful. Many teenagers look forward to their therapy sessions. It's a special time when an adult listens with interest and concern to their ideas and feelings *without* making judgments. Jay is a seventeen-year-old who has been in therapy for eight months. Here's how he explains the experience:

"I look forward to my Tuesday therapy session all week. I know for that one hour I have a captive audience. Dr. C. listens to me and she takes me seriously. She never says things like 'Grow up' or 'Don't talk back.' When I'm angry at her or at someone in my life, I have the freedom to say whatever I'm feeling. Being able to express my anger to an adult without being told to 'shut up' has been a tremendous relief to me. Now I don't hold things in until I feel depressed and confused. Therapy has helped me to feel better on a day-to-day basis. It's also enabled me to understand my friends and my family a lot better. I know that if I stick with it, things in my life will improve. That's because, for the first time, I feel sure that

I'll have the emotional tools I'll need to understand why I do the things I do."

THE PROBLEM OF SELECTION

There are hundreds of trained professionals who can help you deal with your problems. The trouble is, not every one is right for *you*. An important first step in therapy is choosing a therapist who suits *your* needs and *your* personality. If you need help, you might think that your guidance counselor is a logical choice. But take a second look. Do you like your guidance counselor? Do you know him or her? And, most important, do you think he or she has the time and patience to deal with your particular problems?

Many teenagers like to get away from the school environment. They would rather choose a therapist who has nothing to do with school, parents, or teachers. But for most of them, there is one obvious obstacle to this kind of therapy: money. Prices for private therapists can be fairly steep. But they can also be inexpensive. Many therapists have "sliding scales." This means that they are willing to adjust their fee to what you or your parents are able to pay.

If you are reluctant to talk with your school counselor, you should begin to investigate other therapists who are available to you. Before you begin, however, there are a few important facts you'll need to know. Since you will be paying for this service, it's best to be a wise consumer. This means knowing the difference between a psychologist and a psychiatrist and the differences among a social worker, counselor, and psychoanalyst.

COUNSELORS

You've probably met at least one counselor in your life —your guidance counselor at school. But there are also marital counselors, pastoral counselors, and family counselors. Most counselors have a minimum education of a bachelor's degree in counseling. They are trained to help you deal with present problems, such as developing better study habits or breaking up with your girl friend. Community service centers, churches, synagogues, and schools usually have counselors on their staff or can refer you to one.

PSYCHOLOGISTS

Psychologists have more academic training than counselors. They have a minimum of a master's degree in psychology. Many also hold a Ph.D. and can be called "Doctor." But they are not medical doctors and cannot prescribe drugs or give medication. Psychologists are the professionals who perform and evaluate psychological tests. A psychologist might ask you to look at an ink blot and explain what you "see," or to draw a person from an image in your mind. These tests help psychologists to understand more about your hidden fears and fantasies.

Unlike counselors, psychologists don't deal only with

present problems. If, for example, you are having trouble sleeping, they don't just tell you ways in which you might be able to fall asleep more easily. They try to get to the cause of the problem by learning more about your thoughts and your past experiences. Psychologists believe that today's problems are the result of yesterday's experiences.

SOCIAL WORKERS

Not all social workers distribute welfare or are involved in visiting-nurse programs. Social workers function in many different and varied capacities. Many are trained psychotherapists. This means that they have a master's degree in social work (MSW) and at least two years of supervised experience practicing psychotherapy. Social workers have a broad approach toward working with problems. They deal with your environment—the social, economic, and political factors that affect your life. In this way, they are very much like counselors. But social workers also work with the past and with your hidden feelings. In this way, they are very much like psychologists. Most social workers combine these two approaches or emphasize one or the other, depending upon your needs and their preferences.

PSYCHIATRISTS

Psychiatrists are medical doctors who have specialized in psychiatry. They can diagnose illnesses and prescribe drugs. A psychiatrist receives extensive training in psycho-therapy techniques. Many psychiatrists use the "medical mode" in dealing with problems. This means that they will first try to see if your problem is physical in origin. If, for example, you have stopped eating, they might try to find out if you have an illness or ailment that is causing this lack of appetite. They might prescribe medication or tranquilizers. But if the problem isn't physical, the psychiatrist will try to get to the cause of the problem by using the same theories and techniques utilized by social workers and psychologists. This means that he or she will listen to you describe your feelings and then comment or interpret as you unfold your story. Far from being frightening, a visit to a psychiatrist can be a learning experience. And if by chance your problem is physical, the psychiatrist can offer you medical help or refer you to a competent specialist.

PSYCHOANALYSTS

All members of the mental-health profession can obtain further training and become psychoanalysts. The theories of psychoanalysis are based on the work of Sigmund Freud. Freud was the first analyst. He believed that most of our present problems are caused by difficulties and frustrations that occurred in childhood. He felt that we push many of these early memories away and hide them from ourselves.

Our "memory file" or, as Freud called it, our "unconscious" stores all these painful and uncomfortable feelings. For this reason psychoanalysts are not just concerned with present, everyday problems. They concentrate on trying to unlock buried memories and feelings. The analyst believes that this process helps us to learn more about ourselves. In other words, the psychoanalyst believes that our unconscious stands in the way of many of our goals of happiness and success. And by exploring this aspect of ourselves, we will be able to build more productive and satisfying lives.

WHERE AND HOW TO SHOP

Obviously, finding a therapist can be complicated. That's why it's important to spend some time shopping around. Every therapist has his or her own style, technique, and personality. It's a good idea to arrange consultations with three or four therapists *before* you make your final choice. Remember, you will be sharing many of your most personal thoughts and feelings with this person. You must feel that you can trust your therapist. If you go on an interview and the counselor, psychologist, or social worker intimidates you or makes you feel uncomfortable—keep looking. Don't be afraid to ask questions. Find out what kind of training the therapist has had and if his or her fees are negotiable.

If your parents are paying for your therapy, you may have to explain to them that the final choice must be yours. This may take some time, but chances are you won't be happy with a therapist who has been forced upon you. During the initial interview, try to get a feeling for the therapist. Would you prefer working with a man or a woman? Is someone older or younger more to your liking?

These decisions are important. If you feel more comfortable talking to a woman, then look for a female therapist. If older people make you suspicious and dis· trustful, then choose a younger therapist. But what's important is to find someone who is qualified (ask about their degrees), whom you like, and whose fees you can afford.

As a rule, most therapists don't hang out "shingles," or signs, as do doctors and dentists. But just because they aren't as obvious as medical doctors doesn't mean that therapists are hard to find. As a matter of fact, your family doctor can be an excellent referral source. It's possible to ask him or her for a list of therapists without going into detail about your particular problems.

The telephone book is another resource that you should check out. Look under mental health services, social and family services, and community health organizations. These organizations almost always have a therapist on staff or at least a list of names they can refer you to. It's not a good idea just to look up the names and phone numbers of random psychiatrists and psychologists in the Yellow Pages. Try to get a recommendation from another professional, a teacher, a school counselor, or a friend. If there is a university or community college in your area, contact its mental health center or center for student counseling. Local hospitals all have social-work departments that can help you find a therapist.

If you have an urgent problem that just can't wait, a local teenage hot line will suit your purposes. If there isn't one in your area, call the National Runaway Switchboard at this toll-free number—800-621-4000. These people are friendly, sympathetic, and willing to talk to you even if running away isn't your immediate problem. In addition, they can direct you to inexpensive clinics for treatment of drug and alcohol problems, as well as to therapists.

Chapter Ten

ACCEPTING YOURSELF

We hope you've now learned a lot more about when and why you get angry, how to express your anger, and how to look for help if you need it. Emotions *are* strange. They're confusing, upsetting, and powerful. And learning how to control your emotions isn't possible unless you have learned how to understand them.

Anger is an important feeling. It's an indication that something someone has said or done has touched you in a special way. Pushing your anger away isn't the answer. Neither is throwing a wild temper tantrum. But learning to listen to yourself is, because your anger is always telling you something. The message may be expressed in a daydream, an outburst, or a sullen depression. But it's always a message that you need to hear.

Liking yourself means taking yourself seriously and realizing that your emotions are part of who you are. Expressing angry feelings to other people doesn't have to end up in an unpleasant "showdown." When you love or like someone, you should be able to tell them that you're angry, and you should be able to listen to them tell you the same thing. That's what constructive fighting is all about.

If you listen to and accept your anger, you'll gain a life-long friend—yourself.

FOR FURTHER READING

FICTION

Blume, Judy. *It's Not the End of the World.* New York: Bradbury Press, 1972.

Byars, Betsy. *The Cartoonist.* New York: Viking, 1978.

Byars, Betsy. *The Pinballs.* New York: Harper & Row, 1977.

Colman, Hila. *Sometimes I Don't Love My Mother.* New York: Morrow, 1977.

Farley, Carol. *The Garden Is Doing Fine.* New York: Atheneum, 1975.

Harris, Mark Jonathan. *With a Wave of the Wand.* New York: Lothrop, Lee & Shepard, 1980.

Heide, Florence Parry. *When the Sad One Comes to Stay.* New York: Lippincott, 1975.

Holland, Isabelle. *Dinah and the Green Fat Kingdom.* New York: Lippincott, 1978.

Kerr, M. E. *Dinky Hocker Shoots Smack.* New York: Harper & Row, 1972.

Mann, Peggy. *There Are Two Kinds of Terrible.* New York: Doubleday, 1977.

McCord, Jean. *Turkeylegs Thompson.* New York: Atheneum, 1979.

Scoppetone, Sandra. *The Late Great Me.* New York: Putnam, 1976.

Wolitzer, Hilma. *Out of Love.* New York: Farrar, Straus & Giroux, 1976.

NON-FICTION

Bernstein, Joanne E. *Loss and How to Cope With It.* New York: Seabury Press, 1977.

Eagan, Andrea Boroff. *Why Am I So Miserable If These Are*

the Best Years of My Life? New York: Lippincott, 1976.

LeShan, Eda. *Learning to Say Good-by: When a Parent Dies.* New York: Macmillan, 1976.

LeShan, Eda. *What's Going to Happen to Me? When Parents Separate or Divorce.* New York: Four Winds Press, 1978.

Richards, Arlene Kramer and Willis, Irene. *Boy Friends, Girl Friends, Just Friends.* New York: Atheneum, 1979.

Richards, Arlene Kramer and Willis, Irene. *How to Get It Together When Your Parents Are Coming Apart.* New York: McKay, 1976.

INDEX

accidents, 107-09
"acting out of anger," 51-53, 57
addiction, drug, 19, 47, 53
alcoholism, 19, 47, 51-53, 118
allergies, 56
anger,
    acknowledging, 23, 24, 35, 103
    avoiding others', 89, 103
    avoiding your own, 19-21, 103
    cause of, 26-35
    cover-ups for, 46-58
    denying, 14, 19, 21, 48
    disguising, 16
    expressing, 15, 21-25, 36, 38,
      39, 41, 44, 46, 47, 120
    family attitudes toward, 19-21
    fears of, 18, 19, 25, 48, 103
    irrational, 31-34, 35
    old, 12, 27, 29-31, 34, 37, 109
    physical reactions to, 39, 47,
      53-57
anxiety, 47
apology, 93-94
appetite, loss of, 56, 115
asthma, 54-56
attacking, 74, 79-82, 84, 87-88

behavior, defensive, 90, 96, 99-
    100
behavior, self-destructive, 47-53,
    57
boredom, 47

brush-off, 17-18
"buddy system," 44-45
bullying, 19, 24

clarifying issues, 91-93, 96, 99
clown, 24
compromise, 42, 43, 93, 95-96,
    102
constipation, 56
constructive fighting, see fighting,
    constructive
"cool, keeping your," 11-12, 14,
    25
counselors, 57-58, 109, 113
"crazy, going," 30-32, 57-58
crying, 21, 37, 38, 46

daydreams, 28-29, 33, 60-69, 120
    problem-solving, 65-67
    violent, 60, 61-62
death, 105-06 109
defensive behavior, 90, 96, 99-
    100
depression, 20, 21, 47, 49-51,
    105, 107, 109, 120
diarrhea, 56
diary, 35
divorce, 106-107, 109
dreams (nighttime), 67-68, 69
drug abuse, 19, 47, 53, 118

eating, 12-13, 19, 23-24, 47-49, 51

fantasies, 28-29, 59-70
fatigue, 12, 47
feelings, expressing, 15, 43-45, 60, 88
feuds, 73
fighting, constructive, 71-88, 90-93, 96-103
    rules for, 74-88
fighting, destructive, 74, 76-82, 85-86, 88
Freud, Sigmund, 115

goal, your, 41, 43-44, 53, 75, 80
guilt, 47, 62, 89, 91, 94, 107-08

handicaps, physical, 107-09
headaches, 39, 56
help, getting, 109-18
hives, 56
honesty, emotional, 21-23, 71-72
hot line, teenage, 117-18
hunger, 47
hypochondriacs, 54

illness, 47, 53-57

jokes, practical, 19
journal, 35, 68-69

listening, 86, 87-88, 90-91, 95-96, 99-100, 109-10, 120

listing feelings, 43-44
log, 68-69
love, 71-73, 110

memories, 26-35, 36, 37, 84, 115
mental health profession, 109-18
mourning, 105-06

nail biting, 19, 46
National Runaway Switchboard, 118
needs, stating your, 74-79, 86-88, 96
needs, the other person's, 86, 90, 93, 96, 100
negotiation, 43, 95-96
no, saying, 95, 100-02

power struggle, 43-44
pregnancy, unwanted, 51-53, 107-09
promiscuity, sexual, 19, 51-53
psychiatrists, 57-58, 109, 112-15
psychoanalysts, 57-58, 109, 113, 115-16
psychologists, 57-58, 109, 112-15
psychotherapy, 109-18

rashes, skin, 56
role, your, 93

"safety zone," 41-45
self-destructive behavior, 47-53, 57
sex, 19, 52-53, 110

social workers, 57-58, 109, 113-15
"steam, letting off," 37-38
stomachaches, 54, 56
subconscious, 59
sulking, 15, 21
Switchboard, National Runaway, 118

talking, 44-45
tape recording feelings, 44
temper, losing one's, 23-24, 36-41, 42
therapist, choosing a, 112-113, 116-18
therapy, 58, 109-18

ulcers, 54, 56
unconscious, 59, 115-16

vomiting, 56

walking, 44-45
wounds, opening old, 74, 84-88, 99-100, 103
writing down feelings, 43-45

yes, saying, 93-95

"zone, safety," 41-45

About the Authors
Deidre S. Laiken was born in New York City and attended the State University of New York at Buffalo, from which she received a bachelor's and master's degree in education. A former New York City teacher and editor, Ms. Laiken works full-time as a free-lance writer. She is the author of several nonfiction books for adults and is a frequent contributor to *Viva, Self*, and other magazines. This is her second young adult book and first written in collaboration with her husband.

Alan J. Schneider, a native of New York City, received his master's degree in social work from New York University and is presently affiliated with the National Psychological Association for Psychoanalysis. For several years Mr. Schneider directed workshops in emotional education in the New York City public schools. He currently works as a psychiatric social worker for the Veteran's Administration and is in private practice in New York and New Jersey, specializing in individual and family therapy. Mr. Schneider and Ms. Laiken live in Hoboken, New Jersey.

About the Artist
Bernice Myers' cartoon style illustrations have appeared in numerous books for children, many of which she has also written. She lives with her husband, artist and satirist Lou Myers, in Peekskill, New York.